# FOR THE CLARET AND BLUE

# FOR THE CLARET AND BLUE

# AND BLUE

## MICKY SMITH

JOHN BLAKE

Published by John Blake Publishing Ltd,
3 Bramber Court, 2 Bramber Road,
London W14 9PB, England

www.johnblakepublishing.co.uk

First published in paperback in 2009

ISBN: 978 1 84454 780 7

British Library Cataloguing-in-Publication Data:

A catalogue record for this book is available from the British Library.

Design by www.envydesign.co.uk

Printed in Great Britain by CPI Bookmarque, Croydon, CR0 4TD

1 3 5 7 9 10 8 6 4 2

Papers used by John Blake Publishing are natural, recyclable products made from
wood grown in sustainable forests. The manufacturing processes conform to the
environmental regulations of the country of origin.

*THIS BOOK IS DEDICATED
TO MY DARLING WIFE. WITHOUT HER
ASSISTANCE, NONE OF THIS
WOULD HAVE BEEN POSSIBLE*

# ACKNOWLEDGEMENTS

This book is for the many thousands of West Ham fans around the world, those who know what loyalty is – unlike some sets of fans. I would especially like to thank Cass Pennant for all his help and advice.

Many thanks also to the following people who have all helped in some way:

Cookie
Bef
Chris Tye (I got it right this time)
Slackie
Shandy
Stumpy – how's young Bobb (Alex) and Sandra?
Bob the Mod
Jules
Lorna
Heppers
Cloutty
Doddy
All the lads and lasses on the intercyberfirm mailing list

Darren

Digger

Noj, Adele, Nicole, Aimee and Emma

Young Kris (fashion victim)

Porky

Lozza and Monts for being a pair of tarts

Gray from KUMB – great site mate, keep it up

Kiwi Jumbo

All the lads on the Bernard Cribbins West Ham mailing list

Froggy Wicko – hope you get better, mate

Ken at the Sydney Supporters Club

All the lads on the KUMB forum and mailing list

Ashley and Liz

Kev (the under 2)

Anna (wannabe Hammer – don't mention 1923)

Rona (rose)

Guvs (John the quacker)

Fini

Kate (lush)

Geordie Steve

Irish Sean (pastic Paddy)

Debs and Joozis (Pommie Mares)

Manc Karen (Kassa)

Mark and Emma

# FOREWORD

Sitting here in my office, I start to think about how symbolic of modern football my situation is today. A combination of the ridiculous, TV-dictated 12pm kick-off for a game at the other end of the country and my own need to pick and choose away games these days has turned what at one time would've been a 'can't miss' game for me into a complete non-starter.

It doesn't feel good.

Whatever the positive and negative points of today's football, there is no doubting that the sport has changed beyond recognition since the first time I clicked through a turnstile in the 1960s.

Local heroes who you could reasonably expect to run into during the week in your local pub, lads who knew what a local derby meant to the fans and bled for the cause, have been replaced by distant young millionaires far removed from the day-to-day environment and, often these days, the culture of the people who pay their wages.

Satellite and cable TV companies move fixtures around almost at will, the improved quality and depth of their coverage negated by the sheer inconvenience they cause to the long-suffering supporter.

The terrace culture that has been so much a part of the lives of 'lads' for the last forty years has changed beyond recognition too.

Much has been written in the last few years about the subject of hooliganism/terrace culture, some of it from preaching or apologist sociologists, some of it from wide boys telling tall tales, some of it from ex-terrace 'soldiers' or 'generals' whether written by them or through ghost writers.

Some of it has even been good.

One thing most of these books miss – and one thing the commentators, pundits and journalists dare not voice too loudly for fear of being branded soft on 'yobs' – is what has been buried in the scramble to sanitise the people's game for its new middle-class audience.

What has been lost is the game's soul.

The fabulous new stadia in this country have soared ever skyward in the unprecedented building rush that has followed Hillsborough and the later inception of the Premier League, yet all too often these new temples to the people's game are bereft of the very atmosphere and charge that made a weekly trip to the game such a vital part of the lives of so many.

There are too many sterile, regulated and cowed bums on the shiny new plastic seats, overseen by CCTV cameras and police and stewards with almost unbelievable powers of restraint, censure and arrest.

All this loss of liberty and the supporters are paying far too much for the privilege. In what seems a classic case of 'throwing the baby out with the bath water' we have seen what was a necessary and long-overdue change to improve supporters' safety and comfort parlayed and manipulated into a wholesale revolution, one where the ordinary fan has been raped of his and her cultural heritage.

The insidious march of middle-class values and the regulations of successive governments have ensured the success of this revolution, leaving the original fans to either swim with the tide or sink into their armchairs or pub lounges with nothing but a pale imitation of the original match-day experience left.

That, and their memories.

Covering a period of forty years we are taken from the embryonic and rebellious days of the firm through to today's mobile-phone-and-Internet-fuelled last hurrah of what will surely now become a lost subculture.

Using his formidable memory bank and calling on an unprecedented amount of reliable first-hand anecdotes for this project, Micky has weaved his magic again.

Trying to get a true, accurate story of the ICF is indeed a hard task. (For more see Cass Pennant's book *Congratulations, You Have Just Met The ICF.*) Many stories are best left untouched and forgotten. Some may incriminate people. Some are just everyday fans' tales of what they saw on and off the pitch. For this reason Micky has chosen to leave out a few other tales and just add everyday lads that were there, and hopes you will understand.

Twofold.

Yours in Football
Castle Street Charlie
London

# CONTENTS

# THE AUTHOR'S THOUGHTS

Following West Ham United is not about how many pieces of silverware they can win. It's more. With most fans it is a lifelong, sometimes agonising passion. For many it is bred in them and they learn from an early age. It's the small things that count – like teaching your own kids to play Monopoly, telling them that no matter what they must never buy the Old Kent Road and that they will understand in later life.

In the late Seventies I began a new life in Australia with my new wife, probably the best move I ever made, but West Ham was in my blood, rooted deeply in my soul. The coverage of the English First Division by the media in those days was limited – very limited indeed. It was mainly Liverpool games that were seen on the TV, and then only at about 1am or later – and only highlights. Very little of West Ham was seen – in fact, in most cases you would not get the results till the Monday paper. I don't know how much I spent on long-distance phone calls back then. I would ring a friend to find out the result at about 2am our time or even later, only to find out we lost. That wasn't the issue – I just had to know. These days satellite coverage and the internet make life easy when you are 13,000 miles away. Even now my passion for the team has not changed – and never will.

My passion knows no bounds. It was 1980 and we were in the FA Cup final. I was living in Australia on the Gold Coast and my wife was pregnant with our first child. I could not, or did not want to, go back as much as I would have liked to. My wife was insisting that if it was what I wanted then I should go, but I felt I could not leave her alone at that time so I stayed.

The lead-up to the big game saw me decorate the house in all West Ham gear. At work I got invited to an FA Cup party at the local Irish club but knowing the Paddies I declined when I found out that I would be the only West Ham fan there – one Hammer against a dozen Micks did not seem fair as far as I was concerned. I stayed home, well oiled from the drink. I had a mate come around and keep me company. An Aussie bloke, he was not into football, though when the game kicked off he told me he was a sort of ex-Liverpool fan and, because Arsenal played in red, he would go for them. I warned him he had better not be around *if* we lost.

I had the TV up full blast and as it was midnight Aussie time it seems some neighbours had a whine about the noise, especially when Brooking scored. We went on to lift the Cup against all odds and I was in party mood. I carried on drinking all night and phoning everyone I knew in England till the pubs opened on the Sunday, and then till about 6pm that day, until I was blind drunk when – not having the ability to carry on – I went home.

The next day when I surfaced, my wife told me the landlord/real estate agent had had several complaints about the noise. But it did not finish there. My next-door neighbour whined that I had abused him. This I don't recall, but my wife said I told him to piss off 'if he knew what was good for him' on the Sunday after returning home from the pub celebrations. The man was a Man United fan who knew nothing about his side – he once admitted to me he did like Liverpool once but had changed. So all in all your typical glory-hunting c**t. He never stopped complaining to the real estate agent and in due course I was told I was going to be evicted. This did not worry me – in fact, he had done me a favour as we were looking for a way out because we were about to buy our first house. Two weeks' notice was given, which tied in nicely with moving into the new house.

I saw the real estate agent in a hotel in Surfers Paradise about six weeks later. I tapped him on the shoulder and was going to buy him a beer to show no hard feelings, but he went on the defence and gibbered on that he did not want to break my lease and in general made a right prat of himself. He said he could not understand why we 'Poms' got so worked up about a game of football . 'After all,' he said, 'it's only a game.' I shook my head in amazement. He contacted me later on because he wanted some brickwork done on one of his rental properties. So not only had he done me the favour of breaking my lease, he bought me a few beers, grovelled a bit and even put a lot of work my way – all in all, not a bad result. God knows what would have happened if we had lost!

Some of the newer fans I talk to today through mailing lists or chat rooms haven't a clue. In fact, as far as some of them are concerned, being an armchair fan – as some will call you – seems to make you a lesser fan because you don't attend games any more. If only they knew – the passion is lifelong and never dies.

*Micky Smith*

# CHAPTER ONE
# THE AGONY, THE ECSTASY

West Ham United Football Club is an East End of London club, whose fans are amongst the most loyal the country has ever seen. Not the biggest club by a long way, but formed with the workers in the East End in 1895.

Previously called the Thames Ironworks, this small club rose up and not many gave it a chance with company like the Woolwich Arsenal and Tottenham Hotspur, the so-called London big teams. How wrong they were.

The first London team to appear at a Wembley Cup final (known as the White Horse final), when the ground was packed to capacity and then some. The game only went ahead when a lone policeman on 'Billy the white horse' managed to keep the overspilling fans off the pitch. Alas, they lost to the mighty Bolton Wanderers – but it was just the start.

The war final was the next time West Ham played in a Cup final – and they won, but it was dismissed by many as a nothing game due to the war.

After that it was a long time till the next appearance, in 1964, when they lifted the FA Cup with the king of English football at the helm – Bobby Moore, who was the England

and West Ham captain. With a team of many locally bred footballers they defeated Preston North End 3-2 in a thrilling final. It was the first senior game I went to, and what better way to start following a team.

This was to be one of three in a row. In 1965 the ECWC final was won 2-0 and in 1966 England won the World Cup with two West Ham players scoring the goals and the captain lifting the trophy, something no other England captain has ever done since (a lot of people are pushing for Bobby Moore to be given a posthumous knighthood for this effort).

It was a long time between successes. The year 1975 came around and again there was a trip to Wembley and the Cup was lifted in West Ham's favour. We played again at Wembley in the pre-season Charity Shield match but lost to the then-in-form Derby County. A trip to Heysel in 1976 saw us lose the ECWC final 4-2.

Another five years was to pass before Wembley beckoned again. This time we were in the Second Division and played the much-fancied Arsenal. Given no chance against the so-called mighty Gunners, we won 1-0 with local product Trevor Brooking scoring a rare goal with his head. The Arsenal and the football media were gutted – how could this happen? Why did it happen? Many people didn't understand, but came to learn that, no matter what the odds, West Ham fans of the time would never say die. A giant party was on again down the East End. The Arsenal fans were heard to say it did not matter as they were in a European final a few days later (which they lost – and did they moan!).

So what is it that keeps the West Ham fans loyal for so long against all odds? Over the years the board has treated the fans badly and sold off so many good players. We had a name for playing entertaining football, but I'm afraid that doesn't bring the prizes home all the time.

The closest we came to winning the title in recent times was in the mid-Eighties, but even then the hero, Frank McAvennie, was sold to Celtic. No one knew why. He was hero-worshipped and his goals gave us a shot at winning the title for the first time ever. Shortly afterwards we bought him back, when the club was spiralling towards the lower half of the League. Why did they sell him in the first place? This question had so many wondering in amazement.

# CHAPTER TWO
# ONE FAN'S GREAT DAYS

Saturday, May 2 was here. I had not slept the night before, or so it seemed, and I was bursting with excitement. This was the day I was going with my old man and his brothers to Wembley stadium to see West Ham play in the FA Cup final – my first senior game and first ever final.

Normally the old man would not take me to first-team games, only some reserve matches at Upton Park, and then only if I behaved. But this was different. He wanted to go to the semi-final at Hillsborough against the Busby Babes and made a deal with Mum that if we made it through he would take me to the final no matter what. It was on. I remember listening to the squeaky broadcast on the BBC to see if we had won – we had. In the rain and slush we had beaten the Busby Babes 3-1. I was over the moon. I could not hide my pleasure and was out on the street cheering and carrying on. And I was not alone. Most of Burdett Road was doing the same. We were at Wembley, our opponents Preston North End. No problems for us, we were gonna win the Cup.

The old man came home late that night, very late, and I was told to stay in bed. I could not wait till the morning when I could find out all about the game. The highly fancied Manchester United were picked to win the Cup that year and West Ham were given no chance. But young Johnny Sissons, Ron Boyce and Geoff Hurst made sure we went through. Now Wembley was next.

In our house nothing else was talked about but the upcoming final. Loads of kids round our way were also going and those who weren't were jealous of those of us that were – and we rubbed it in something rotten. We played games over in Victoria Park and there were always fights about who was West Ham and who was Preston, then more fights to see who wanted to be their favourite player no matter what.

Anyway, back to the final. On the day I was up at sparrows' fart, Mum wondering why I could not get up as quickly on school days. She was amazed! She would be glad when it was all over and said she could not bear it if we lost. Not just because she was West Ham as well – she said it would be like a funeral parlour round home if we lost.

Dad had tickets, his brother had arranged them, and we were over the moon. The big day came and my dad met up with his mates outside his local, which opened early on the day. As a kid I had to wait outside with the mandatory crisps and lemonade, with instructions that he was not to be disturbed as they were planning the day and would not be long. It seemed ages before they all came out and off we set towards Mile End tube station, my uncles bunging me a few bob on the way. In fact, if I recall rightly I had nearly 30 shillings, a small fortune in those days and an even bigger one for a kid my age. I was chuffed!

At Mile End there were many West Ham fans all dressed up in a variety of claret-and-blue colours, home-knitted jumpers, you name it. Loads were singing 'Bubbles' and as we got aboard the train it seemed to be full of joy as nothing else was mentioned but bringing the Cup home. The semi was talked about, and as a kid your ears tend to flap a bit so I picked up a few things. Being a naïve kid, I never realised until later on in life that they were talking about the crowd trouble that was starting to happen, even back then.

Every stop up to and past Liverpool Street station, more and more West Ham fans were piling on. The carriage was packed. Many had half-bottles of rum or whisky, and one lot had a crate of beer. Everyone was happy as we changed lines to head to Wembley. I could not wait.

The old man gave me instructions for if he lost me in the crowd – I was to get the tube home and wait at his local, he would not be far away – or better still go home and tell Mum he was not far away. He told me how to get home but was shocked when I told him a better way, and quicker. My days of bunking off school and riding the tube all day had its advantages! Being brought up in the East End made you street-wise. God help you if you weren't.

We got out at Wembley amid a massive sea of colour and people greeting us – I was so excited. There were programme sellers, rosette sellers, hat sellers, you name it. My old man bought me a scarf, which I have now entrusted to a mate who I know will look after it – but more about that later. Those silly hats with two colours, like trilbies, were all the rage – and a con according to my old man, who would not buy me one. I had forgotten that I had money, so I bought a big rosette instead, 2/6d I recall. 'Bleeding con!' was the cry from my uncle, who told me you'd only pay 1/6d down Green Street for it. 'Bloody spivs,' he remarked; he even wanted to take it back. I had to wait for what seemed hours outside the Greyhound pub while they went in for a drink, but it wasn't long before they came out, with comments like 'Bloody toffee-nosed prices, this ain't the West End!'

The noise around me was unreal. The sound of the sellers shouting, the mounted police horses clopping along, the cars trying to get through the mass of people. We walked down to the ground and finally got in and I could not believe the size of the stadium and the number of people coming in. West Ham fans were drinking from half-bottles they had sneaked in and it wasn't long before 'Bubbles' went up as the band played their own version and the crowd sang along. This set the tone for the day. Many a West Ham voice could be heard calling out now, mainly having at pop at Preston. Many times the crowd seemed to all laugh at the same time. The atmosphere was great now. There was the sound of breaking glass as another empty half-bottle was finished and dropped on the terracing. The smell of drink was all around, the mandatory peanut shells everywhere and claret and blue all over. It had to be seen to be believed. Little did I know then this was to be the first of many journeys for me to Wembley, but this one was special.

I was raised as a West Ham supporter; all my family were West Ham with the exception of my brother, who for some reason chose Wolves – I still dunno why to this day – but he soon changed after that final. Most of the family would not talk to him about football and many times me and my other brother were called upon to sort out a row with other kids or to back him up as he was always getting the mickey taken out of him. Kids down our way were unforgiving.

The national anthem was played, the royalty met and it was warm-up time. Nearly three o'clock, only a few minutes to go, but it seemed like eternity for me. I remembered my granddad telling me about the 1923 final – how he walked to Wembley that day with the crowds and how the crowd spilled onto the pitch. I tried to imagine it but the whistle blew for kick-off and it was back to the game.

I could not distinguish all the players and had to look at the numbers of both sides to see who was who. At Wembley behind the goals you are a fair way from the pitch and as an eleven-year-old I found it hard to follow. My old man put me in front of a crash barrier right by the upright and I was told to stay there all game as it was safer. I found out what he meant later on. With the sway of fans the pushing and shoving going on was unreal. I remember the crowd going deathly quiet as Preston scored. It was like someone had died. Moans about having played John Lyall's testimonial match days before were going around – people were saying we were tired and that it should never have been played.

If I remember correctly when the half time break came we were 2-1 down. The young Johnny Sissons had scored the first and when Geoff Hurst levelled it up in the second half the West Ham crowd went potty; it was unreal. Hurst had scored in every round and had just done it again. At 2-2 the game was a thriller. I was finding it hard to keep up but then Ron Boyce slipped home the winner and I will never forget the roar of the West Ham faithful. There wasn't long to go and the final whistle blew at last – WE HAD WON THE FA CUP!

People were going mental, hugging and kissing. My old man was nearly crying and I was jumping up and down. A chorus of 'E-I-A-D-E-O WE WON THE CUP' burst out, quickly followed by 'Bubbles'. It was so loud! Bobby Moore lifted the Cup and celebrations were of the extreme. Bobby was named 'footballer of the year' that season. He was loved by all West Ham and you would never hear a bad word spoken about him.

After about an hour the crowd was thinning out. I had lost the old man or he lost me, I dunno. I finally got out of the stadium and headed to the tube. People were still celebrating, dancing around, singing. The Greyhound pub was packed – no good looking for the old man there, I would never find him. I headed home. The tube was full of singing West Ham fans. A few Preston lads were on the carriage I was on. There was no trouble, a bit of gentle banter and hand-shaking mainly. Back at Mile End and outside the station the pubs were packed and had people spilling out on to the pavement.

I went home to find the old man had beaten me home, picked up Mum and headed down to Green Street to celebrate. My brother told me he was off too but that I had to stay home. Yeah, right! I was out like a shot, meeting my mates and going over the game time and time again with them, showing off my new scarf and rosette. I was the talk of the street amongst our lot of friends – what a way to see your first senior game!

I went to a few more reserves games after that but they seemed tame. Even the odd time I was taken to see the first team it still was not as good as the final crowd but a lot louder than the reserve games. I got to see a lot of first-team football from then on. I saw two European games – Sparta Prague and the semi-final of the ECWC playing Real Zaragossa in a packed Upton Park.

## CHAPTER THREE
# WEMBLEY AGAIN

We made it through to our first Euro final again at Wembley, playing TSV Munchen 1860. I really wanted to go to this one and the old man kept me dangling. I made sure all the odd jobs were done around the house, kept my shoes clean, offered to clean the old man's boots, tried to stay out of trouble at school and at home and when I finally got the nod that me and my older brother were going as well I went mad. Nearly a year after the last final I was to make the trip again, but things were a little different this time. The old man knew I could find my way around all right and me and my brother were to meet him at the Two Puddings pub at Stratford at opening time. We found out later that it was open nearly all day.

I was raring to go, this time scarf ready but no rosette. I had flogged that for a quid at school – not bad money in those days, but as it turned out the kid who bought it had done his gas meter in to buy it and got into all sorts of trouble. He never told why he wanted the money. If he had, my final trip would have looked shaky.

We finally left Stratford and got the tube to Mile End and

changed lines again. The trains were full of West Ham fans and many seemed more confident this time. The old man gave us our tickets, a sign to us that if we got split up we could get in OK. A few bob each from him and our uncles and we were set.

Arriving at Wembley station we lost our old man and uncles, or they lost us, but we did not care. I was 'Jack the Lad' at this lark now and showed my brother the way around once inside the ground. My brother and I got some light ales at one of the bars. He was older, and if asked said the drinks were 'for Dad, mister'. We had about four to five small bottles I remember, then some barley wine. I felt funny and don't recall much of the game except we won 2-0 and we were going potty. The Cup duly lifted, songs sang, we made our way home, a journey which seemed to go on forever.

Back at Mile End the scene was the same as the previous year – people going mad all over. I felt sick and was worried what would happen. When I got home Mum was there and asked what was wrong. We said we had eaten one of those hamburgers you could get at the game (you know the ones – a piece of rubber between a stale flat roll slopped on with a ton of semi-cooked onions) and had felt bad since. She gave us a funny look. We were hoping she could not smell the drink on us. Thank God for Bazooka Joe bubble gum! She made us a cream soda with milk and packed us off to bed saying we would be OK by the morning. I don't know what time the old man got home but found out later that he came and got Mum again and went down East Ham way to my uncle's place.

The next morning we made our way on to the Mile End Road hoping that like the year before the Cup-winning team would come along there showing off their Cup. Once there we knew they would be coming as thousands of people were milling around. Some looked like they just got back from the game, singing, mainly drunkenly, cheering, loads dancing. It was a funny sight. I have often wondered how many did not show up for work – loads it must have been, but no one seemed to care.

West Ham had won the ECWC only once. It had been won once before by Tottenham. This was a mainly all-English affair with local lad Brian Dear scoring both goals. I have watched the game many times on the telly years later and still believe it was one of the finest Wembley finals ever. Champagne football, that was what West Ham were known for – the entertaining Hammers – and how true that was. I had been to my second final in as many years but little did I know I had a third coming up, a game with which many Hammers fans claim – and rightly so – that West Ham won the World Cup. I went to Wembley many times in later years after those three games to see other finals, but it was never the same atmosphere that I had felt at the West Ham finals.

I went to the 1967 all-London final and to say I hated it would be a fair statement. I went again in 1973 and that was quite good but the noise and atmosphere was nothing compared to the 1964 game.

There wasn't much fighting in those days. The odd punch-up but nothing like the organised carnage that swept the game for years to come. I saw a fair bit at the 1967 final but nothing to write home about.

I knew that West Ham were the team (and supporters) for me. They were all I knew and loved. It was reared in me – from my granddad, who went to the first Wembley final, right though to me and my brothers. When my brother supported Wolves for a while I recall that my uncles kept asking my dad what he did to make him that way – and, indeed, I overheard him saying he did not know where he went wrong, such was the loyalty to West Ham in our family. To even think about following another side, like the double-winning Tottenham, was not on round our way. A few kids did, but they paid for it big time in the end, only being allowed to join in games of football or cannon now and then. They were prime targets for crushing tackles and the like.

We used to play over in Victoria Park against kids from Roman Road, whose area took in Bow Boys School – a bitter enemy, as our schools hated each other. It always ended with some kid from both sides steaming off in tears, saying, 'I'm gonna get my big brother' and so on. If a kid played who was not West Ham he would be last to be picked and very rarely made it through a game without copping a dead leg tackle or a big sliding tackle that saw him fly up in the air. No one cared and many laughed – he wasn't West Ham and he did not count. It was after many of these tackles and this treatment that my brother saw sense and became a Hammer. The games got better for him from then on and we seemed to have less fights with the other lads.

## CHAPTER FOUR
# FIRST GAME ON MY OWN

My first game on my own was against the Busby Babes in 1967. A big game for them, because a win against West Ham and they would have clinched the title. That day was madness on and off the pitch. (For more on this read *Want Some Aggro?*, by Cass Pennant and Micky Smith.) I knew my father was at the game with his brothers but did not want me around. As a fourteen-year-old I deemed I could look after myself, which I could in a fashion. The events that took place that day changed my life forever. Indeed, they did so for many an older West Ham fan as well, with many swearing never to go back to football again. The age of the football hooligan was here.

Some say an advertisement was placed in the local paper the, *East London Advertiser*, saying that the Manchester boys were coming to the East End to show what a night on the town was. I don't know if this was true or just an old wives' tale, but judging by the people at the game something urged it on. What happened that day made headlines around the country. The game would never be the same.

Still smarting after their 1964 semi-final loss, the

Manchester fans sought revenge and the many thousands travelling down to London got some – but not as easy as they would have hoped for. On the pitch they flogged us 6-1 to clinch the title. Attitudes changed towards them. They had some respect after the Munich air crash and many an old boy round our way admired the way they had rebuilt after that. After 1967 any respect they had went out the door and it hasn't changed to this day.

Over the years I have followed West Ham up and down the country. I have been abroad to Heysel to see us lose the 1976 ECWC final – Lampard (arrrrggghhh!) and Van Der Eldt, who later played for us, killed us. The then mighty Anderlecht on their home ground were too good. I was hoping for another double like '64/'65 but had to make do with just 1975 this time. The 1975 final was really a boring game to me, now I was a lot older and wiser (well, I thought I was).

I watched as Fulham were beaten by us 2-0. Alan Taylor ('Sparrow') was the hero as in the previous games against Arsenal and Ipswich in the semi. The crowd was just as potty then but half a skinful of drink in me made the afternoon more enjoyable. I remember my mum telling me not to eat one of *those* hamburgers, with a wink in her eye. I guess you can't fool your mum as easily as you think you can. The fans engaged in a giant piss-take: one banner read 'West Ham 2, Dads Army 0', referring to the older Fulham players like Mullery and our Bobby Moore, who had left us to join Fulham at the end of his marvellous playing career. This was his first year at Wembley again, but not as captain. Many felt sorry for him, but it soon passed. The final whistle and we had won. The fans went crazy and invaded the pitch. It had been a decade since we had won something and we had steam to let off. Some said it was to fight the Fulham fans. That was rubbish – it was just the sheer pleasure of having

16

won. It was about twenty to twenty-five minutes before the Cup was lifted and the West Ham fans went spare. It was party time.

I still had my scarf from the 1964 final with me and had bought another one at that game, an away one based on the Manchester City 'sort of' theme scarf. Many older fans will know what I mean. I must have looked a sight with two scarves tied around the wrists, Bay City Roller-style, but who cared – we had won and it was party time.

After the game many headed off towards Trafalgar Square. We joined in for a while, then off to Green Street. On arrival the place was packed right down to the ground. People dancing, cars could not get through, many just left their motors and joined in, which added to the chaos. We managed to get a few take-away beers in the pub opposite Upton Park station. We could not get near the Boleyn and the Queens was packed out of the door, but who cared. It was party time!

I have been lucky enough to see four Wembley finals with West Ham, if you count the 1966 England game as having been won by us (which I do). With the 1964 match being my first senior game I feel I am more lucky than some. I still love my team with a passion, even after living a large part of my life in Australia. As I said earlier, it was hard in the early days to get any information here on any English football. Sometimes it was Monday's paper before you could get the results or maybe a Sunday drink with other ex-pats to see who had heard anything. Now with the Internet and Pay TV it is great and a lot easier to follow your team.

When I think back on how the game has changed since I left, I think of the rip-off prices for season tickets the modern-day fan has to pay. I'm told most of the crack has gone, it's all so sterile now the all-seater stadium is here. It's no longer a working-man's game. The East End has changed. Gone are most of the traditions now. In come the -isms – racism, fascism, feminism etc. It's another world. So when people say I am not a supporter – just a fan, a part-timer, because that's what the dictionary says – because I don't go any more, I think, Yeah, right. They will never see what I have seen live, and anything they will see I will watch from the comfort of my own home without paying the rip-off prices the clubs demand from ordinary punters. So I stay a part-timer if that is the case. Now I am nudging fifty I doubt if I will see West Ham live again. My reasons are simple: I retired at 45 and was then told I had MS (Multiple Sclerosis) and was going blind. So my life is sort of restricted now. I still enjoy what I can and when I go totally blind *then* I'll start worrying about it. Until then I keep sorting my old West Ham stuff out and earmark a lot of it for mates in the UK, who I know will look after it. The 1964 scarf (as I mentioned) I have already given to a good mate who I have never met but I know he is West Ham through and through, one of the old school, and he will pass it on no doubt to his kids. My kids were born here and while they know how to hate many teams it's hard to explain the love of West Ham. They know I am potty about them and my daughter proudly wears my West Ham tops to college. She knows who Bobby Moore is but, alas, that is it.

My collection, built up over the years, is going to good homes. Some to Toronto – to Stumpy, who has already got some. Others to Bef, a solid West Ham lad, and a few of the bits and pieces I dig up around the place to other people. Bobbie the Mod has some Sixties badges to go with his fashion of the time – hope you enjoy them, Bobbie. Basically that's it, my life as a West Ham fan. There is loads more I haven't included here but I have tried to keep this book about the uniqueness of being a West Ham fan not about anything else.

## CHAPTER FIVE
# DIGGER'S TALE

I never really had a choice in the matter, even if I had wanted one. Being born and raised in the Barking and Dagenham area, if you liked football you were West Ham – simple. I can't remember anyone around me supporting anyone else. As a little kid I'd see the older local boys come home from Upton Park walking in gangs and singing, and I could feel the envy growing inside me and wish that I was old enough to go with them. That's what it was about: belonging.

You don't choose West Ham, it chooses you. If it were just about picking a winning football team you'd pick Manchester United, Liverpool or Arsenal instead of a team where you never knew whether or not they were going to be relegated or maybe get promotion. One year they're playing out of their skins to get a draw from Chelsea or Spurs and the next season you have the delight of seeing them play Grimsby or Barnsley or even losing 5-2 against Tranmere Rovers in the cold and the rain. But you know you'll be back to see it all over again. If nothing else, it gives you a great sense of humour – what other supporters would sing, 'We're going down, we're going down, you're not, you're not'?

But everything would be forgotten at the sight of a Tony Cottee goal. The South Bank would erupt as one and surge forward. People would go over in the rush and someone they'd never seen before would pick them up and they'd jump up and down together. And who could forget such sights as Martin Allen scorching through the midfield and letting go with a thirty-yard screamer into the roof of the net, or Julian Dicks going into a crunching tackle and picking up the poor attacker by the throat. It would make the hair on the back of your neck stand on end.

Without a doubt we have the most vocal and loyal supporters in the country. Everyone remembers the FA Cup semi-final at Villa Park with the non-stop chanting of 'Billy Bonds' Claret and Blue Army', but the atmosphere was similar at all games. If it started to go a bit quiet, a quick shot of 'North Bank, North Bank, give us a song' would get the ball rolling again. The feeling of getting off the tube at Upton Park and walking down Green Street (sometimes down the middle with the traffic forced to a standstill) towards the Boleyn for a quick pint or six would make you nervous with anticipation. Then, leaving the pub with only ten minutes to spare, the noise coming from the ground would grab you by the scruff of the neck and pull you towards the turnstiles, a lot quicker than you would normally walk, for a quick frisk by the local constabulary, and then you're in and taking your place just before kick-off. The sheer noise of shouting and singing would give you such a buzz you knew why, win, lose or draw, you would be back to do it all over again.

The date is December 12, 1992. I had a date with an Australian girl and West Ham were at home to Southend United. The game was obviously going to be another 'classic' that I could not afford to miss, so I asked her if she'd like to come along. She generally hated all sports, but after I convinced her that there would be no trouble at the match she agreed to come. She couldn't believe what was happening. The amount of people walking down Green Street, the singing and dancing on the pool tables in the Boleyn and then what was happening inside the ground. We stood in front of a crush barrier, so she wouldn't get knocked about too much, and next to us was a bloke with a young kid of about three or four on his shoulders and they were both singing 'I'm Forever Blowing Bubbles'. I think we won 2-0, or 2-1 – the score didn't matter, it was magic on the South Bank that day and my date enjoyed the atmosphere so much she made several trips back. We later married and moved to Australia in 1994.

Not long after I emigrated, West Ham had a summer tour Down Under and were due to play at Lang Park, the home of Rugby League in Queensland, and just down the road from where we live. Of course, I had to go. When I got there I could not believe my eyes. The place was awash with claret and blue. I've no idea where they all came from, as normally the only football shirts you see around here are Man U or AC Milan. A rather large person walked by the section where I was and was greeted with a chorus of 'Who ate all the pies'. And this was Brisbane, not London E13! When the West Ham side was announced I only knew about two of the players. I think most of the first team were pissing it up on the Gold Coast. I can't remember who we played (I think it might have been the Australian Under-19 side or something), but I know that we lost. Same old West Ham.

So what about now? People are always asking me if I miss home and I say that the only things I miss are my family and friends, West Ham and decent pubs. Most people then say, 'What are West Ham?' Now I rely on TV and radio coverage, and keeping in touch over the phone and Internet. But I'm still a passionate supporter, and, in fact, probably spend more time on West Ham-related things now than when I was back in England. I'll be over at the end of the year for a holiday, and of course a visit to Upton Park. Am I a glutton for punishment or what?

## CHAPTER SIX
# MANNYGATE

If ever a saga truly summed up the agony side of being a West Ham supporter, then Mannygate was it. I have seen West Ham knocked out of Cups by all manner of reasons over the years – abject surrender, refereeing blunder, bad luck – but this administrative cock-up was a new one even for us. For once we had done the business on the day, only to be denied by an off-the-pitch cock-up that saw an ineligible player take the field. Did he smoke the winner in? Did he make a last-ditch tackle or score a crucial penalty in the shoot-out? Nope – he was on the pitch for six minutes and touched the ball briefly twice. Emmanuel Omoyimni – I couldn't even spell his bloody name until this incident. Now no West Ham fan will ever forget it.

Three things still grate with me even today. The first is Doug Ellis, Chairman of Aston Villa. Our error was stupid, but innocuous and had no bearing whatsoever on the result of the match. He was on about us cheating and, when the FA eventually caved in, the cheeky sod said, 'West Ham should be grateful they are still in the competition at all.' Second was the fact that you knew that, had Manchester United or

Arsenal committed a similar offence, they would still have progressed to the semi-final. Ferguson would have gone purple with rage at the mere thought that his side would be denied their rights by such a meaningless error, and the FA would probably have given them a bye to the final to compensate his hurt feelings.

But by far the most galling aspect was the Tranmere-Sunderland FA Cup tie that happened a couple of weeks later. Tranmere were hanging on with a 1-0 lead when one of their players was sent off. As he departed from the pitch, Tranmere brought a sub on! This 'extra player' then made a crucial headed clearance in the last minutes. So West Ham had an ineligible player on the pitch who made two irrelevant touches, whereas Tranmere had an extra player on who made a decisive clearance. You'd think that would make Tranmere's error more serious than ours, wouldn't you? You might, but the powers that be didn't. The Tranmere result stood, and the ref got a slight rap on the knuckles. Manny's two irrelevant touches rendered the whole tie void, and we had to replay.

The first Villa match itself was one of those wild West Ham games that make you think, This club is going to kill me. At the time West Ham were flying, and Villa were in a run of diabolical form. Thus, you'd think we'd have torn into them from the kick-off to exploit their fragile confidence and impose ourselves. However, we sat back and Villa scored first after five minutes. We slowly stirred, and by the last fifteen minutes were pounding away at the Villa goal and grabbed a crucial equaliser soon after. The game looked set to enter extra time when, with a couple of minutes to go, Dion Dublin cracked home a stunning volley. Twenty-three thousand West Ham fans sat muted in shock and disbelief. But, with the ninety-minute mark long gone and the ref poised with his whistle, Kitson was bundled over in the box and we got a highly dubious penalty. Amid crackling tension, Di Canio drove the penalty low to the keeper's right. It was the last kick of normal time. After a fairly insipid extra half-hour, we entered a penalty shoot-out. Di Canio started well, driving his penalty low and hard to the keeper's right. Then, tragedy struck when Sinclair missed our third kick, and yet again we stared down the barrel of defeat. But Alan Wright and then – inevitably – Gareth Southgate missed for Villa, and we went home in utter delirium. We could almost smell the silver polish on that elusive first trophy for twenty years – Leicester, a team we did the double over that season, waited in the semis, and Tranmere emerged from the all-First Division other semi-final to provide final opponents. It was to last just 48 hours ...

The feelings of dismay and despair when the Mannygate story broke were hard to take. To have something that you already had taken away was unbelievable. I remember the feeling that we would never win a trophy again. It's very hard to say who was at fault. The company secretaries resigned, but you wonder why Redknapp, whose policy it was to loan players to lower-division clubs, didn't know or check with Manny. Or why Manny didn't stick his hand up and say, 'Er boss, I did play for Gillingham in this Cup whilst on loan, are you sure I'm OK to play?' To compound it, Redknapp, when asked why he brought Manny on, said, 'I don't really know why I brought him on.' So our best opportunity for silverware goes down the swanny courtesy of a substitution that had no reason or logic behind it. Tremendous. So very West Ham.

By the time of the replayed fixture all West Ham fans were fervently hoping that we'd put Villa away again. Then, in about fifty years' time, maybe we could have seen the funny side – 'Hey, do you remember that Villa quarter-final? Two matches for the price of one, and we're the only team ever to win a trophy having won the quarter-final twice.' However, reality had to intrude and our defeat in the replay condemns Mannygate to the Hammers Hall of Horrors for the rest of time. In truth, Villa, buoyed by their unexpected and undeserved good fortune, had begun to find form, whereas our shattered team had begun to struggle.

On the night itself, we had opportunities to win but did not take them. We took the lead soon after half-time with an excellent Lampard lob, and were within minutes of the final whistle and a 1-0 win when Taylor equalised for Villa. Minutes into extra time Taylor got another, and we were 2-1 down. But we got another penalty, and Di Canio stepped up. Now, note my description of Di Canio's previous two penalties against Villa in this tie. Low and hard to the keeper's right. Perhaps he thought that he'd double-bluff James in the Villa goal – surely he'd go to the other side, and thus by going right again the keeper would be fooled. If that was his plan, it did not work. James dived the same way that Di Canio had put his previous two penalties and, lo and behold, there was the ball to push away. Villa added a third, and the fat lady broke into song.

You can always look back and find turning points in a club's history. We turned for the better when we signed Kitson and Hartson in 1997, which saved us from relegation and saw us start a run of three seasons in the top half, plus the Intertoto run. This may turn out to be a negative turn. At the time of the first Villa victory we were on a great run of League form and were, of course, in the semi-finals of the Worthington Cup. After Mannygate, our form fell away and we missed out on a League European spot as well as the chance of UEFA Cup football via the Worthington Cup. Villa revived and went on to clinch an Intertoto spot. Had we, say, gone on to win the Worthington Cup and clinch a UEFA Cup spot, then that summer may have been very different. The Cup final cash, plus a UEFA Cup place, plus a higher League finish may have seen Redknapp given a few more million to spend over the summer, and seen us as a more attractive club to come to. Perhaps Rio would not have made his mind up to leave, resulting in us finally accepting Leeds' £18 million a few months later. Perhaps a nice UEFA run would have seen us not needing Leeds' £18 million, and telling them to fuck off. We will never know. But this will always be one of my darkest episodes in following West Ham Untied FC.

# CHAPTER SEVEN

# WITHIN THE RANKS: A FAN'S JOURNEY WITH THE ICF

These stories were put together following my reading of Micky Smith's excellent recollection of his early hooligan days following West Ham United. It struck me that, as Micky was leaving for Australia, I was about to arrive on the scene with the 'younger lads' that Micky was referring to in his accounts.

I never considered myself as 'a top boy', or indeed a ringleader in any of the events described. But I was there and recognisable to a lot of well-known faces of the time. I'm sure that many who were around during this period will empathise with the feelings of the time and will probably recall some of these incidents – although everyone has a different version of events, depending on where you were and what side of the road you happened to be when things kicked off.

There will be opposing supporters who will possibly disagree with some of these events or even recall other events that may have happened. But if I wasn't there it wasn't fair of me to include them in these short stories. I have tried to be honest in my recollections but time does cloud your memory of certain moments.

I don't personally think West Ham, or any other club for that matter, will ever be able to recreate this unique period when each big club had a sizeable mob and were often taking it to other clubs/towns/cities across the country on a monumental scale.

These stories are not a chronological account of each season and I found it easier to dedicate sections to certain teams rather than researching stats or fixtures.

In the beginning: I was born and raised in London's East End, which was a good place to build character and make you street wise from an early age. My family were all East Enders, with my dad coming from a large Canning Town family and my mother hailing from Stratford. I spent most of my formative years around the streets of Canning Town, Plaistow, Custom House, Upton Park and East Ham.

Although it sounds like a sketch from *EastEnders*, you could actually leave your front door open in those days and neighbours were always popping in and out of your home without ringing the bell or knocking on the door. You looked after each other round our way and, although there was many a family dispute and blows in the street, you always sorted it out and ended up having a few beers in the local. Kids were always playing football in the road and I can only recall my childhood days with affection – never a sad time.

But it was difficult if your face did not fit or if you moved into the area from outside London. Northern and Scottish kids were often targeted for abuse, but those that could handle themselves soon fitted in with the locals. The schools were very rough, the kids poorly educated (most of it was down to the kids rather than the teachers) and anyone who went to Woodside, Cumberland, Eastlea etc. will know what school days were about back then. You quickly formed a pecking order among the males (and females, for that matter) and you formed relationships with a certain group of mates and stuck by them through good or bad times. I still keep in contact with kids I first met when I was in my pre-school nursery in Stratford.

We lived in a small three-bedroomed house, even though there were six of us fighting for space, and this was not untypical of other households in the area. Most of the households did not have bathrooms and you had to go along to the communal baths for anything more than a 'top and tail' in the sink. We also had an outside loo, which was freezing during the harsh winters we had back then. You didn't hang around longer than needed back in them days.

We were very family orientated. All of my dad's family (there were six of them) visited my nan's house in Canning Town every Sunday without fail. The adults would sit around eating and drinking, whilst all of the kids (there were eighteen of us) would run around the streets playing games like 'run out' or 'bull frog'. We were always getting into trouble for making too much noise or running through other people's gardens and even climbing on the garage roofs around the estate where my grandparents lived.

My dad and his brothers were all West Ham through and through and were regulars at home games, which was a short walk away from our home. In fact, I could see the West Stand roof and floodlights from my house and I could hear the roar of the crowd on match days.

I can still remember being in the street and being fascinated by the hordes of men making their way to the ground. They always seemed to be so happy and excited and I longed to be able to go too. We often 'looked after' the cars in our road and got a few quid from the owners in return. In

31

reality you stood by the car until they were out of sight, then you went off to play for a few hours until around 5.45pm. Then you all rushed back and waited for the owners to return and for your reward. I'm sure they knew this anyway, but it prevented them getting a nice scratch or a flat tyre. Extortion began early in the East End.

I will never forget one Saturday when we were about six years old and one little cheeky beggar who lived down our road approached a newly parked car and demanded some money from the driver for looking after the vehicle. The owner pointed to the window and said, 'Take a look in there, sonny,' pointing to a big German Shepherd in the car. 'He is more than capable of looking after my car for me, thank you very much.' To which this urchin replied, 'Well, I hope the fucker can blow tyres up, mister,' before running off to avoid a clip around the ear.

England had just won the World Cup (a memory I sadly fail to recall as I was a tad too young) and West Ham were becoming popular. They had won the FA Cup in 1964 against Preston North End and then defeated Munich in the 1965 ECWC at Wembley. What with Moore captaining the World Cup winners and Hurst and Peters scoring all four goals, West Ham were on the crest of a wave. Forty thousand packed into Upton Park every week back then and this Greenwood era seemed to be the making of the club.

Unfortunately, the club failed to build on this success and the coming years were pretty non-eventful for the regulars. In E13 there was pretty football and a feast of goals but sadly it always seemed to end in defeat. However, the support was local and these guys were very loyal to the club and continued to turn up week after week for their weekly dose of torment.

My first visit came towards the end of the Sixties and I was hooked. The noise, the smell – peanuts, hot-dogs and the tobacco – plus this fantastic swaying crowd of men moving to and fro and side to side in a continual motion. I was transfixed by the events around me on the terraces rather than the playing field and this was probably true for the years ahead.

My dad and his pals would stand on the South Bank terracing and the kids all stood on crates or boxes next to the crash barriers – a new feature at most grounds following the Ibrox disaster, which I can still recall hitting the headlines that fateful Christmas.

The First Division, as the top division was back then, contained some strange teams compared to today's Premiership. I can recall the games against Burnley and Huddersfield, who were all top-flight teams. Wolves had a very strong side, with the likes of Derek Dougan, Willie Carr, Parkes, Hibbit and Parkin, and I can recall some good games against them at Upton Park.

On occasions my dad could not take me and I began to go with some of my other family members – uncles, cousins etc. – and they used to stand on the West Side near the South Bank. I loved it there far better than the South Bank and I was always disappointed to return to the South Bank whenever my dad took me.

Around the age of seven or eight, I was able to go along without my dad and there were quite a few kids from my school that would go too. Little did I know back then that I was about to succumb to the lure of the hooligan. One of my school mates came from a very large (and rough) family in Plaistow. His elder brothers were always in trouble and I tagged along with this kid for a few games. I was attracted by the fact that his brothers were often nicking scarves from opposing supporters, which was the done thing, and he would turn up at school on a Monday with two or three fine examples of other club scarves. The silk ones were the business, more sought after than the woollen ones, and we often stood amazed, looking at these in the playground.

The South Bank was always known as the away supporters' end and I don't remember too much trouble there towards the end of the Sixties and early Seventies. I can recall games against Man United and Liverpool where, from the front of the South Bank, you could look back and see hundreds of scarves held aloft during a rendition of 'You'll Never Walk Alone' and I was completely gob-smacked by it all. I was grabbed by the footballing bug and nothing was going to stop me. There may have been trouble and fights going on, but I certainly don't remember them happening.

My first insight into this violent world was against Newcastle United. I don't recall the score or the scorers but I left the South Bank (which had a few hundred Geordies in it) and was about to make my way home when I bumped into my mate from school. He was standing with his elder brothers and about two hundred other shady-looking characters outside the main exit of the South Bank in Castle. I asked what they were doing and he said they were going to do the Newcastle fans. Great, I thought to myself, I'll stay and watch and maybe grab my first scarf.

As the Newcastle fans came down the steps leading out, a shout went up and this West Ham mob just ran at them, scattering them everywhere. Some tried running back up the steps but they were being pushed back down by those at the back who wanted some action – not realising how many nutters were waiting for them. It was complete chaos and there was no police around to quell the violence, which seemed to go on for ages. I failed, in my trance-like state, to even attempt to grab a scarf, but I had seen my first big football row and I was excited by it all. I wanted more.

We talked about this in school on the Monday and more kids wanted to get involved and grab scarves. As for me, I wanted to know what the plan was the following week and how many supporters were expected down. My mate and his brothers were a great source of information – some of it grossly exaggerated, when I look back. I was in love with West Ham and I longed for them to do well. But the fighting seemed to be the second best thing and if you had a shit result you could always look forward to watching the older boys cane the away fans in or around the South Bank.

There was no such thing as crowd segregation in those days. In fact, there didn't seem to be that many coppers around to sort out the disturbances that were becoming more and more frequent. I began to hear of stories where West Ham had gone to other grounds in London and had had right results, taking liberties and fighting on the home ends at various places. My mate had gone to some of these games and I was dead jealous, as my old man was not about to let this youngster travel halfway across London on his own. My dad knew that trouble was brewing (he had seen it first-hand on his trips to Old Trafford and the like) and did his best to steer me clear of this growing trend.

I was playing regular football at this stage and I lived for Saturdays. I was playing for my school team two years ahead of my time (my dad had been a semi-pro and could have played at a much higher level if it hadn't been for injuries) and I could not wait to play on a Saturday morning. Another lad I grew fond of was an outstanding footballer and his dad was a keen football follower (although he had a soft spot for Chelsea, I later discovered). If West Ham were away from home in the afternoon, this other lad's dad would take us both off to the Os at Brisbane Road or even another game across London somewhere.

The first was against Coventry City. They brought a few hundred down and I was fascinated to watch them singing and then storm across the stand at the final whistle for one of the ends. The second game was against Millwall (I did not know they would become such fierce enemies over the years to come), and I can recall them having Harry Cripps playing for them – a real hard man that won the applause and respect of the visiting Millwall fans. They were a boisterous lot at Brisbane Road that day and I remember thinking how similar they seemed to the West Ham mob I was beginning to recognise.

I also copped a day out to Stamford Bridge (it was the glamorous year, post-FA Cup success) and they had a marvellous team then – Osgood, Cooke, Harris, Webb. I think Chris Garland was a new arrival back then. We sat in the West Stand and I was mesmerised by the noise and unruliness of the large mob stood to my right on the Shed End. When the game ended I asked my mate's dad if we could exit the ground via the Shed End. I wanted to stand on that terrace and take it all in and be a part of it.

I watched the final against Leeds on the TV and had been cheering them on like mad (David Webb was a local East End lad and I kind of felt an allegiance towards the Blues), but even then, at a very tender age, I made the decision that it was West Ham for me. They were my local team, they were family, and I wasn't too impressed by all these Nouveau Blues that seemed to have appeared out of nowhere following a little bit of success. I felt there were too many Johnny-come-latelys among them with their fresh new scarves who had no idea what the club was all about. The attraction of the King's Road and the 'Swinging Sixties' all seemed to make it the club for those outside my class group and I wasn't wearing any of it.

## *THE EARLY AWAY DAYS*

I was into secondary education before I began going to London derbies and I was often taking the cheapest route possible. I would bus it with a few mates across to Tottenham or Arsenal, changing two or three times on the way. The bus would always fill up with our opponents' fans and they would often be of a similar age. Quite a few times it would kick off and we would chase the kids off the bus or even get chased ourselves. Nothing too serious – a couple of whacks and a grab to begin with.

I recall one of the games at Highbury and being on the Clock End, which was a vast open terrace. It had kicked off on the North Bank all afternoon and West Ham and Arsenal seemed to be having a go at each other – with limited success, due to the vast number of police in there. We were trounced on the pitch 6-1 and we left before the final whistle for the bus journey home. I bumped into my mate and he told me one of his brothers was slashed across the back and had had his jacket ripped during the fighting. Although not in the same league as West Ham for wanting it everywhere, Arsenal were a handful at home and always defended their North Bank with pride. We did get some good results in there and I never witnessed anyone bringing it to Upton Park on the same scale on a regular basis. I gradually came to believe that we were the biggest and best firm around, even if we did cop a hiding from time to time.

Despite the way a firm appeared, there were always occasions when you could come unstuck against the most surprising of teams. In the ensuing years I was to see West Ham get taken by surprise by a number of teams, and I don't hold the notion that we were unstoppable or immortal in any way. You have your good and bad days, but generally West Ham seemed to get more results than others and they were as game as fuck wherever they went. They did not seem to have too many who would have it on their toes at the first sniff of trouble and would nearly always stand and have it out no matter what the numbers or the likelihood of copping a real beating. These were your mates who you grew up with, and no one wanted the reputation of being a runner or a coward. You stood by them no matter what.

I suppose it was around the mid-Seventies that I had first heard the term 'Inter-City Firm'. It had become a powerful number of troublemakers who had decided to give up the football specials and travel outside the boundaries imposed by most clubs. Most people wanted to travel on organised coaches or trains, but this lot wanted that little bit extra – to travel undetected, at times that suited them, to enjoy a beer, without the attention of Old Bill. A lot of firms preferred the football special because they knew it guaranteed police protection if it all came on top. Even though they would shout the odds and get lippy from behind the safety of the police escort, they were content to have large numbers, all singing, and say they had taken it elsewhere. But the 'Inter-City Firm' had gone one step further and were becoming a feared force. When West Ham were in town, you could guarantee there would be some action and most clubs looked forward to the visit and the chance to pit themselves against this increasingly famous mob.

My early impressions were that this mob of older lads were game lads too far out of my league and I wasn't sure I wanted any part of it. But the kids at school were often picking up the ICF chants and making out they were part of this fearsome mob, even though it was clear they weren't.

At the age of fifteen or sixteen, I decided that the new season would see me on my first away game outside of London. With a mate of mine we walked down to Laceys coaches in the Barking Road at East Ham and paid our money to book ourselves on the first game of the new season – Leicester City. I did not know what to expect. My mate had a huge Union Jack with West Ham in painted white letters across the middle and we were on the coach early to drape it over the back seats in full view. I was excited and apprehensive, not knowing what to expect on the mid-week journey. The coach drivers back then had strict instructions to arrive very close to kick-off to avoid rival firms being around the ground for hours prior to the game starting.

It was clear to me a few of the lads on the coach were maniacs – they were talking about what they were going to do to any Leicester fans they met. I thought it was best for us to stick around these lads rather than walk around on our own. After a few long hours we arrived. It was close to kick-off and as the coach slowed though the city traffic we abused every passing Foxes fan we could. Most laughed, as they did not fancy fifty nutters jumping off and steaming into them, but one or two reacted, only to run a mile as soon as someone got up to get off the coach.

We were dropped off outside the main stand and kick-off was just a few minutes away. We followed the nutters around the ground to what we thought was going to be the West Ham section (which used to be a small part of the little stand to the left of the main stand as you look on to the pitch). But as we entered the ground it became obvious we were in the Leicester end, which was at the other end of the stadium. I quickly tucked my prized West Ham silk scarf inside my Harrington jacket and kept quiet. The nutters had quickly met up with some of their pals and were towards the back of the stand to the left-hand side. I recall seeing a tunnel to our left that led from the main stand into the end we were in and you could see people walking back and forth. All of a sudden the teams appeared and a big chorus of 'Bubbles' went up from around us. We were suddenly under a hail of flying debris – stones, bottles, coins and I had my jacket up around my head for protection. I could not see out of it but then heard a huge roar (that unmistakable sound when a mob makes a charge) and as I appeared from the safety of my jacket I looked around to see a huge gap on the terrace to my right. The West Ham lot just steamed into the Leicester firm and sent them running for cover. From the tunnel on our left we saw more West Ham lads pouring though from the main stand and joining in the mêlée. Chaos ensued for what seemed like hours, but was probably only a few minutes. My mate and me singled out a group of lads our own age and landed a few blows in the name of West Ham. It had been my first real taste of action and I was proud to be a part of this growing movement.

I think the game ended in a 1-1 draw, but I could not wait to get back to my mates at home and tell them about what we had been up to. We were buzzing all the way home on the coach and I got to bed very late that night. I was still at school and had little or no money and I had to wait until later in the year before my next excursion, which was Coventry City. I seem to remember it being on or around November 5, because we jumped off the coaches near the ground and the Old Bill had us all against the wall searching us for fireworks.

We were in the away supporters' section, which was an open terrace, and we spent the whole game abusing the Sky Blues fans to our right on the other side of the fencing that was there. Coventry scored first and their fans went mental, but we reacted by lobbing anything we could find over the fence. Then a couple of skinheads in front of me lit up some 'bangers' and launched them into the Coventry fans. As they exploded the Old Bill went berserk and charged into our ends trying to find the culprits. They were pushing and shoving and a lot of people got upset and started attacking the police, who quickly withdrew. It must have been frightening being a copper entering our section of fans like that with a few hundred angrily shouting, 'Kill, kill, kill the Bill!'

West Ham equalised and our fans went ballistic once again. More fireworks were lobbed over the fence but the police had learned their lesson and stood down the front looking up at us all. One or two were nabbed and escorted away but there was no sign of trouble inside the ground. Coventry was always a good trip for West Ham as it was quite a short trip up the M1 or by train and we always seemed to get a result up there on the pitch. As I became more involved with the modern ICF we never really had much opposition up there, although it could come on top of you if you wasn't careful. They always allowed you in their boozers, behind the away end as well, which wasn't the same elsewhere in the country.

I know some lads who took liberties behind the Coventry end one year and got a slap, but we often chased around after them with little response. One season we all sat in their end behind one of the goals in the downstairs section but they did not do a thing. On another occasion we were only about ten- to fifteen-handed walking around the ground when we met a little firm of them coming out of a pub behind their end. They followed us down a short alleyway at the corner of one end and we kept on walking, but making sure we knew how many there were and just how close they were. We decided that once we reached the end of the road we should all turn and just run at them, do or die. We saw about thirty to forty of the fuckers. 'Come on then if you want some,' we shouted, and the whole Coventry lot had it on its toes. Not impressive!

We took over pubs and ground when we went up there for the first leg of the League Cup semi-finals in 1981 and took the piss completely. We lost 3-2 after leading 2-0 and we were gutted all the way home, thinking we had blown it. They brought a lot of fans down for the second leg, but not much of a firm and we beat them by a single goal by Jimmy Neighbour to reach Wembley for the second year running after the 1980 FA Cup final win over the Arsenal. We went wild that night and looked forward to the final with the Scousers.

### OFFICIAL ICF – THE NEW BREED ARE HERE
#### Within the ranks

In my late teens I had heard from a friend of mine that the ICF were to arrange an 'official meet'. I can't recall if the original 'Inter-City Firm' had died a death and they wanted to restart it all or whether it was a fresh new legion of young recruits coming through. Anyway, the deal was that they would have all these calling cards with 'Congratulations, you have just met the ICF' on them and they were going to leave them on their victims. The plan was to meet up at Mile End station one Saturday morning (West Ham were at home that afternoon) and to travel on the tube to Euston and King's Cross and catch as many mobs as they could. There would be London firms going up north and lots of northern firms coming down to London and they had one thing on their minds – carnage.

I was working and unable to meet up in the morning, but by all accounts they dished it out to all and sundry that Saturday. They even did a group of northern rugby fans who were in town for a big game and they left them battered and bleeding. This was the new breed, a mixture of young lads in their early twenties or late teens and far different from the earlier West Ham mobs I had seen. They were cheeky young fuckers who were always up to no good, but there were some very, very funny people amongst them. The word spread and the numbers grew very quickly.

This West Ham mob of the mid-Eighties had grown rapidly and was formed by three elements. There was the older lads who had been giving it for years and were now in their thirties, then there was this new group of lads in their early twenties who had emerged and, finally, the younger element (sixteen- to seventeen-year-olds), who would later be known as the 'Under-Fives' because of their young age and looks. The first time I had heard the term 'Under-Five' was when we took a little mob for a nothing youth game at Millwall. We had a bit of a result and took some liberties with Millwall and were enclosed in the halfway stand made famous by the 'F-Troop/Harry the Dog' documentary.

Some of the older lads were mucking about fighting with the younger lads and started calling them the Under-Five firm, which seemed to stick. I don't know for sure that this was how this term came about, but it was certainly my first recollection of it. There was some naughty lads in the Under-Fives and a lot of them liked to carry blades. I still know a lot of the lads today. Some of them could handle themselves in a row, but a lot of people were wary of them back then because they hunted as a pack.

A few of them weren't all that good in a one-on-one row, but as a unit and with weapons they were deadly and would often leave their victims in a bad way. I think the fact that most had older brothers was part of the problem. Some of these older brothers were as hard as nails and a handful for anyone. The younger lads had reputations to keep up and made up for their lack of strength with the fact they were tooled up and weren't afraid to use what they had. Most of this mob came from the Custom House and Canning Town areas and they were always seen as a group at away matches within the main mob.

The ICF could easily muster a mob of three hundred to four hundred for the right game and there was very rarely less than a hardcore two hundred for most games. Although it was mainly local lads from East London and Essex there were also a number of others that came from far and wide. Glaswegians, Welsh, Norfolk and Suffolk, Northerners and people from the suburbs of Kent and Surrey could all be found within the firm and I personally knew loads of lads from these areas.

I never ever fathomed how so many people could find out about a time and a place for a meet-up, but it happened. Mile End was always a favourite place for meeting up before away trips as it combined the District and Central lines on the tube and was accessible for everyone from all areas. I would always know the time of the meet and the intended train we were going to catch out of Euston or King's Cross and so did everyone else. Someone always knew someone who had the details and word spread like wildfire among the West Ham lads.

You would be looking through the fixtures months ahead and trying to work out who you could meet on the tube or at the British Rail stations around the country. New Street in Birmingham was always a good place for bumping into another mob, if we were heading further north and they were heading for the Smoke. I spent my youth living for the next weekend. The ICF was probably at its peak in the early Eighties, when we were back in the Second Division. That season saw an awesome mob cause havoc around the country and the following few seasons after promotion were equally exciting.

At the time, I was drinking around Stratford of a Friday evening, which was probably the busiest place around Newham for a night out, with a choice of many pubs and clubs at the time. People often frequented the 'Two Puddings', or Bobby Moore's pub, which was a business venture for the late, great player. But there was always trouble around the place every weekend. Little mobs from Canning Town, Stratford or Custom House would declare war on another little group and it would kick off inside the boozers with pint glasses flying everywhere. These people knew each other and would have little retaliations over the coming weeks, though everything seemed to be forgotten the next morning when you all stood side by side for West Ham.

Everybody had little scams going to get cheap rail tickets at the time. The 'student railcard' was available to everyone under the age of something like 24 (and you did not even have to be a student) and it gave you half-price travel anywhere. There were also people travelling on 'family railcards' – you could buy one full ticket and get four or five tickets at just a pound. The younger lads would go as kids and you split the cost between five or six of you – it was peanuts.

Fellow travellers who had the misfortune to be on the same train must have hated it. As soon as the buffet opened everyone dried out the buffet bar buying as much beer as possible. You were just topping up from the Friday night, although there were those that did not consider the drinking side of the day – they wanted clear heads.

The main faces within the ICF were known as the 'guvnors', men who had earned their reputations on the streets. You all knew them, who they were, and they often orchestrated events. I will not name anyone but I think most people who have seen the *Hooligan* documentary will understand to whom I am referring. Certainly most West Ham knew them. The police tried to round them all up following that video but made some serious mistakes in their prosecution, which resulted in all the cases being thrown out. This was the beginning of the end of the ICF, though, and most boys wanted to keep their heads down for a while.

I still see a number of lads at Upton Park, and indeed away games, but they tend to hang around in smaller groups and they are there to enjoy the football rather than chasing opposing supporters all over the place. I still believe that the emergence of widely available drugs had as much impact as the introduction of the all-seater stadium in terms of things easing off. We were often drinking in the West End in our own little group on a Friday evening. It was nice to get out of the East End but we were always bumping into little mobs from north or south London up there. There was always an atmosphere in the pubs and clubs and it did not take much to spark off a big row. You could feel the tension when you walked into a club and saw another little team in numbers – you knew who they were and vice versa.

But when the House music scene kicked off towards the end of the Eighties and early Nineties, everyone was doing Es and the mood was noticeably different. The people who had wanted to hit you for who you supported a few months before were now all over you like a rash and talking all sorts of bollocks. But no one cared and it was actually a refreshing change to be able to have some sensible (well, almost) conversations with some of your former enemies.

Before this I wouldn't dare admit to, or even entertain the thought of, having large groups of Arsenal and Spurs fans with me, but I go drinking with all sorts now and apart from a bit of good-humoured banter it never gets heated. It used to be very different. Back in the heyday of the ICF I was working with a girl who had a flat in Stratford and she was having a party one evening. She'd invited loads of people from work, and they came from all over the place. One big lump, an Arsenal fan, was all mouth and claimed he knew all their boys and hung around with them. I once saved him from a right hiding when West Ham were chasing Arsenal around Euston station. He ran past me at full speed with about six or seven Gooners being chased by a large mob of West Ham. As he approached me I shouted, 'I'll have him ...' and was about to unload one on him when I realised it was the Gooner from work! The other six kept running and I told him to stay with our little lot. The other West Ham came running out of the station asking if we'd seen some Arsenal and we said they'd just sped past us heading down the main road towards King's Cross. This Arsenal lad breathed a big sigh of relief and said he owed me one (cheeky shit). Anyway, he was due at this party in Stratford one fine Saturday evening in the summer and the meeting place for those who didn't know the area was a nearby pub that just happened to be the Britannia – a staunch West Ham pub that was owned and run by Frank Lampard.

I later found out at the party, from others that were in the pub, that the Gooner bowled in the joint, complete with red home shirt, and was very quickly approached by one of the regulars who insisted he remove the offending shirt or 'fuck off to another, friendlier pub'. He had no choice, as he didn't know where the party was, so he removed his shirt and sat quietly in the corner, much to the amusement of all those present – priceless!

I happened to be working in south London at this time and was friendly with a number of good lads – some were Arsenal, one or two Spurs and a few Millwall lads who were good blokes. One was scary-looking, with a big scar right across his eye from top to bottom, the result of a glassing that left him partially blind. He was actually a really good lad, not as fearsome as at first appeared, and we often swapped tales from our respective weekend adventures across the country. I think West Ham and Millwall had a mutual respect for each other (not that we'd admit that at the time) as we were basically very similar – very poor areas which were built around the now-defunct docks. Wide-boys everywhere offering you everything from a joint of meat for your Sunday dinner through to TVs and sofas in every pub on every corner. Both mobs were fearless and very rarely backed off or ran, even when the numbers may have been against them. I, for one, had a nervous, gut-wrenching feeling each and every time we headed over to the Den. You wanted their mob, but you knew that they weren't going to have it on their toes and you could very likely cop a hiding if you weren't careful. I'm sure a lot of their lads felt the same on their visits to east London.

## IT'S A LONDON THING

The derby games in the capital were always interesting and it was easy for little groups of you to come unstuck if you happened to bump into the main mobs while you were walking around. So I'm not going to start with a league table of who was harder than who because everyone had their results and also came unstuck. I can honestly say in all my years I can still only remember two firms who dared to enter an area other than the away section of Upton Park

The first was Tottenham, who turned up in the North Bank in the late Seventies. They took a bit of a battering and were quickly escorted out to their own end – but at least they had a go. Then in the mid- to late Eighties I recall a mob of

Arsenal led by a certain black guy entering the lower West Side (it was all seating) and giving it the big one. It was mainly scarfers and old boys around when they sounded off, but people jumped on to the pitch, which made it look like they were having a right result. As soon as we rounded up a little firm to have a go back they quickly jumped the walls and walked back to the Arsenal end of the South Bank. But fair play for trying it.

It was probably harder for the likes of Millwall to do something similar, as the police presence for West Ham/Millwall games was astounding. I have a lot of respect for Millwall and if you ever met a decent firm of them you knew it was going to kick off. I expect most people have now seen the British Transport TV documentary that showed our lot turning up mob-handed and doing them down the Old Kent Road in their pubs before one such game.

On another occasion – and during the summer riots in Brixton, Toxteth and Moss Side – West Ham drew Millwall in the Southern Junior Floodlit Cup final, which was a youth tournament. The game was to be played over two legs. I told my Millwall pals at work that we intended bringing a firm over and they were laughing at us, saying we would get slaughtered. It was around late April near the end of the season and we arranged to meet at Mile End. We did not have a massive mob, maybe a hundred to a hundred and fifty, but they were nearly all top boys.

We took the District, then the East London line to New Cross. I remember one of our lot clocking some geezer who got on the train purely because he was a south Londoner. Some of the West Ham lads pulled him up and told him he was out of order and that they would be looking for him at the front of our mob when it kicked off, otherwise he would cop a hiding from them on the way back. He just replied, 'I'll be there, don't worry yourselves.' We poured out of the station and straight into the pub across the road, but there was only the old boys drinking in there. We then came down the hill and turned right into a park. There were some young Indian lads playing cricket so we nicked their stumps and bat as weapons and carried on through the park. We had been clocked, by sheer coincidence, by a patrol of SPG Old Bill who thought we were on the riot. We told them we were going to the football but they would not believe us because they said they would have known if a game had been on.

They followed us from a safe distance behind. We walked on and were intending to turn right behind Cold Blow Lane End. We came underneath a railway bridge and we were right upon them. The game had just started, but a few of their boys were outside the ground. A shout went up and we steamed into them only for Old Bill to drive through the lot of us and swing the van between the two groups. They drew truncheons and kept us apart until reinforcements arrived.

By this stage the Bushwhackers were pouring from the terraces and were there looking at us outside their end, having took liberties. The police eventually put us in 'The Half Way Line' and we spent the game exchanging verbals about the incidents at Bank and King's Cross stations. I was suddenly aware our group had halved. Some of them had got an escort and went roaming. That left about sixty to seventy of us and the Old Bill just put us on a train and sent us packing.

We fully expected to meet Millwall at Surrey Docks or one of the other stations en route back to Whitechapel and we knew they would be mobbed up and angry. We then made sure we all got on one single carriage and we stripped seats, lighting tubes, the handles with the balls that you hang on to, etc. In fact, anything that could be used as a weapon. The train stopped at Surrey Docks for ages and we suddenly realised that one of the passengers that got off had probably informed the Old Bill or Transport Police that we had wrecked the train.

Someone spotted the Old Bill arrive and we quickly set about putting back all the stuff we had removed. As the Old Bill came down the steps on the opposite side of the station and then around on to our platform they found an immaculate carriage with the whole lot of us sat down. Putting on fake posh voices we asked them, 'Excuse me, officer, do you have any indication when this train will be continuing its journey north?'

Nothing happened for the rest of the journey and I walked into work the next morning and slaughtered the Millwall lot, who were highly embarrassed and promised an even better show the following week for the return. West Ham were all mobbed up for this. We had hundreds around Upton Park and in every pub and bar, walking the streets, checking the underground, but they never showed. I turned up for work next day and they said they did, in fact, meet up and had about a hundred or so. They decided it was not enough and they would have got caned, but then again that's what we took over there.

It got really nasty between the two clubs during the attack on some of our lads at the Bank tube station. I'm not sure of the full story other than they jumped a train full of Millwall's firm. I heard they were attacked with knitting needles and broken glass, but some Millwall lads who I knew said they took liberties thinking they were only a handful on the train when, in fact, it was a whole trainload, not one carriage. Either way they got turned over badly. One lad was stabbed seriously and went to hospital but some of them made it back to Euston to find the rest of us on our way to Villa. Everyone was fuming, but we decided to sort it out later.

We took it out on Villa first, after sitting in the stand opposite the main stand right up next to the Holte End. We came out afterwards and ran their lot ragged all the way to Aston station. Then it was back to London to sort out Millwall (who were up north somewhere like Doncaster). We got back to Euston and travelled on to King's Cross. The OB were out in force and were asking us to point out the people we thought had been involved!

I've never seen West Ham so up for an off. As their train slowed into the platform, we poured down the concourse at them. A lot of them were expecting a reaction and had jumped out and were running back towards the lines. It was sheer chaos as West Ham were just grabbing guys and kicking them to bits. I saw one group of about five West Ham lads absolutely slaughtering some poor fucker on the ground. The OB arrived and the lads pointed him out as being one of the people involved, so the OB nicked him! The OB generally hated Millwall and let us take liberties that night.

There were repercussions for weeks after, and one small mob of West Ham went over to London Bridge one Saturday morning (we were at home ...!) and tried to catch little pockets of them heading off to an away game (they may have had Stoke). They found one lot of Millwall and ran them outside the station before launching a petrol bomb that exploded against the station wall.

Another time, we were heading somewhere up north from Euston and Millwall were playing someone up north and departing from St Pancras. We came out of King's Cross tube into Euston Road and found a handful of them. They had bags of beers that they were stocking up from an off-licence for their journey. Some of the older West Ham lot knew who they were and gave them a hiding (we were about 150-handed). But these game fuckers got up off the floor and asked for more!

They walked fifty yards down the road towards St Pancras and were shouting, 'Come on then if you think you're hard, West Ham.' So another lot ran at them again and gave them another hiding. This happened two or three times until suddenly we were outside the big steps from the station and about three hundred of the fuckers came pouring out at us! They took us by surprise and it was the one time I witnessed West Ham retreat and have it off down the road. They chased us down Euston Road until we stopped outside the fire station. People were screaming, 'Stop, you fuckers. We're West Ham, stop and have it,' until everyone stopped, stood and then charged back at them. This surprised them a bit and we gave them a go back. But the OB arrived and moved us back to Euston, where we met Arsenal and gave them a bit of a slap as they tried to jump on their train to Coventry.

Spurs, Arsenal and Chelsea all had their moments but at that time I'd say that West Ham and Millwall were definitely the boys. The biggest difference for me was that we had intentions of finding them all, home or away, whilst they only put up a solid show at home. They often brought numbers to Upton Park but they never really did too much to avoid the OB and the inevitable escort to the ground.

To highlight the point, we were going up to Sheffield Wednesday one cold Saturday morning when we were told the game was off. It was the 1980/81 season from what I can remember, and we were well mobbed up for what was going to be a big day out (you didn't get too many big teams in the Second Division back then). We decided it would be a shame to waste such a good mob and so we looked through the Saturday papers for a good London game to attend. We found it: Spurs at home to Liverpool.

We headed for White Hart Lane and about two hundred to three hundred of us arrived down Tottenham High Road around midday. The Old Bill were not ready for us, and neither were Spurs. As we came to the Corner Pin pub we ran a mob of them and they were on their toes like a flash, thinking the Scousers had turned up mob-handed. We wanted to get on to the Shelf but, after fun and games running around the ground, they finally caught up with us and told us they were putting us in the Park Lane terraces and we were sandwiched between the Scousers to our left and the Shelf to our right.

The Liverpool fans could not believe what was happening and we spent the whole afternoon taking the piss out of the Spurs lot. The game was televised on *Match of the Day* that night and we took great delight at hearing the choruses of 'Bubbles' during the game.

Before I finish with London clubs I have to say that the death of an Arsenal lad (name withheld out of respect) in that fateful game at Highbury changed my view on the Gooners. We often ran them around stations and at Upton Park and also at Highbury, but they put a good show on that day. We were in the North Bank early but they sussed us out and steamed little mobs of us early on. I was eventually taken out by Old Bill and put into the stand to the right of the North Bank as you look towards the pitch. Then, near kick-off time, it erupted and a decent West Ham mob were into action on our left. An orange smoke bomb was let off to increase the chaos and a good off ensued. The Old Bill kept the two sides apart but the Arsenal probably would have got on top otherwise.

After the game we roamed the streets and there were loads of skirmishes going on everywhere. We eventually boarded a train that was heading back into Arsenal station. Their mob lay in wait to ambush us but they did not think we would be up for it. We steamed off the train and they ran through the many long tunnels under-neath the station. I quickly boarded the train again with some mates, not wanting to engage in another long chase, as we were already knackered. It wasn't until I got home that evening to our pub in the East End that my mates told me someone had been stabbed to death. I know a lot of our lot were rounded up and questioned at length, and someone may have even been charged at some stage. But I don't think anybody actually got sentenced for the lad's death.

Knives were a very unwelcome part of the scene as far as I am concerned and the stabbing of another fan was nothing to be proud of in my eyes. There have been so many deaths that have occurred at football – a Millwall fan, an Arsenal lad then a West Ham lad, at the Monument station to name but a few. Some people may disagree and say it's all part of the scene, but each to his own.

### ANGELS OF THE NORTH

I think the rivalry in the Eighties between West Ham and Newcastle was probably as fierce as the Millwall thing, with several incidents adding to the cause. I remember one occasion when we were waiting for the Geordies to come out of Upton Park in the early Eighties. There were hundreds waiting for them by the Boleyn pub to have a go at their lot heading for the coaches. The police often struggled to contain this back then, as we were on both sides of the road and it was chaos everywhere.

I read in a local paper that a squaddie (Newcastle supporter) was badly beaten and had lost the sight in one eye in a skirmish after the game when a minibus full of Newcastle lads turned into a mob of West Ham in one of the back streets. It was the following year that we went mob-handed expecting a rough time – and we got it.

Our train arrived early but we had been split up purposely by the Transport Police at King's Cross. Many of my mates missed the train and had to get a second train, but we had a sizeable mob as we pulled into Newcastle. We poured out of the station and the Old Bill weren't ready for us. There was a bar right across the road – it might have been a Yates's – slightly to the right, with a little firm outside. They were different up there, and they weren't into casual clothes, brand names etc.

They were big hairy bastards, loved their colours and were as hard as nails, but we steamed into them and there were glasses going everywhere. We turned left and then came across another boozer full and had it with them, giving them a bit of a hiding. We then marched through the shopping centre giving it to all and sundry. Windows were being smashed, and we were really up for it. As we got rounded up and marched to the ground somebody told me that a petrol bomb had gone off outside the ground aimed at West Ham. I didn't really believe them, and thought it was a bit strong.

The lads on the second train got a real hiding. The Geordies had dusted themselves down, licked their wounds and were now mad as wasps in a bottle. One of my mates had his nose broken as his lot were ambushed by Newcastle. Inside the ground the atmosphere was tense and midway through the first half someone lobbed a bottle into our section. It hit the deck and burst into flames. I was shell-shocked.

I don't know if anyone was seriously injured, I don't think they were, but West Ham were now seething. At the back of the terraces were some portaloos and they were right next to a small fence that separated us from the Geordies. You daren't go for a piss or crap for fear of being hit by hundreds of missiles being launched from either side of the fence.

A year (maybe a couple) later, West Ham fans were banned

from St James' Park. West Ham refused to accept any tickets and said we'd be turned away if we arrived at the ground. There were no Football Specials or coaches and the OB were going to be out in force at Kings Cross. So we hired a fleet of minibuses and made our way up there – about a hundred and fifty of us.

We stopped on the edge of Newcastle and parked the buses up before making our way to the ground – there was no way they were going to keep us out and even if they did we would have made an impact! We encountered a few little mobs of them on the way in and it kicked off a few times. The OB did actually let us in – it was all a ploy – but there weren't many of us in the away section. We were escorted back to the minibuses afterwards and I later heard that one of the minibuses pulled into a service station on the outskirts of Newcastle and were met by some mouthy Geordies – who didn't realise this was the ICF! One of them was 'borrowed' for the journey home apparently, and pleaded for his life, fearing they were going to do him. He had no money and had been moaning that he was due at a family party that evening in Newcastle and had no way of getting home with just a few quid in his pocket. They let him go just outside London and I don't know what happened to him after that.

On another occasion I was late out of bed one Saturday morning when we were due to play at Leeds. This was a big one and one of our first encounters with the growing LSC[Leeds Service Crew] on their manor. I ran for the train at King's Cross and jumped on as the doors shut. The train only had about fifteen to twenty West Ham on it, and I asked if any of them had seen the main mob. They told me they were catching the next train up – *BOLLOCKS*!

I decided I would get out at Doncaster and wait for them there, grab a bite to eat and a coffee to get rid of a ridiculous hangover. I was walking around Doncaster on my own, the other lads on the train had also got off and were sat in the station buffet. I walked along one of the many platforms as a train started pulling in … it was full of Newcastle's top boys on their way to somewhere like Grimsby! I shat myself. It was too late to run anywhere and I just had to blag my way through it if possible. I got some strange looks from them; they knew I was a Cockney by the dress code and they thought I must be a football fan. Two or three of them came over and asked what team I was. I said I wasn't anything to do with football and was meeting a few friends to go away for a few days up north.

I managed to escape their attention, although they were not convinced by my story. They followed me at a distance and when I looked across the platform I saw the other lads from the train getting a good kicking. I wandered down another station platform and was hoping that the ICF mob would arrive in the next fifteen minutes and meet this lot so we could get at them. I felt uneasy and was obviously next on their list for a hiding. I walked down the platform as another train pulled in to my right and the little firm who attacked my fellow passengers were heading my way straight ahead. I could not bottle it, I had to front it and act as normal as possible – *WHERE WAS THE ICF TRAIN?*

I thought the lot in front of me were about to head my way, when one of them spotted some Leeds lads on the newly arrived train. They all leaped on board and caned the Leeds fans, leaving me with a safe passage down the platform. I still had a few of them on my tail and was hoping they would join in the Leeds bashing. Suddenly their mates were shouting that the connecting train was there and they began to run away from me – *phew*!

As their train departed, loads of them were looking through

the windows and I felt obliged to give them the wanker sign. Within minutes of them departing our train pulled in and it was packed to the rafters with top boys. I found my mates and they could not believe how lucky I was and how unlucky they had been at not meeting the Geordies. That would have been a massive off, with little or no police presence.

When we got to Leeds station we expected a full-on police presence and a heavy escort. They'd need numbers as we were firm-handed that day, three hundred to four hundred top boys all wanting to know what all the LSC fuss was about. A policeman with a loudspeaker gathered us together and told us we could make our way to the ground, with no escort, but to keep out of pubs as there could be trouble! We couldn't believe our ears. We made our way to the ground, passing loads of little mobs of Leeds who wouldn't dream of having a go at us with our numbers and no OB.

We passed several pubs with loads of them looking out of the windows and then headed down some road and across a footbridge across a main road. We had it there with a small mob of Leeds and then headed for the ticket office at their end of the ground. We all bought tickets for the Leeds section, and about two hundred of us got in there among them. This was in the days when the away fans sat in the small terracing in the side stand and Leeds' mob sat behind the goal next to you. But here we were, in their end, expecting a real battle.

Close to kick-off they started coming in the ground, to be met by a big ICF presence in their stand. A big shout of 'Bubbles' went up, which prompted more of them to pour into the ground, but there was nothing they could do. The OB made a line between the two of us and kept us apart, but we'd come up here and taken the piss as far as we were concerned. Each time someone went for a pee, you'd get up and then two or three of them would get up and go down from their side. So another four or five of your lot would follow and it went on like this all afternoon – very amusing, really.

I know some lads that have had a hiding in Leeds and don't dispute the fact they can deliver the goods on the day, but we had got a result there on that occasion. The following season, I think (or maybe the same season), we were out in force at Upton Park waiting for the LSC. The pubs and bars outside the station were packed and we had numbers that day. Little mobs of them arrived and were escorted to the ground, but we had been told that day they had a big mob in town from our spotters. We all agreed to wait for this big mob before making a move. It got to 2.55pm and no show. The police on horses and the dog handlers all began moving on to the ground, but we stayed hoping that they had stayed as a mob and had not got by us in small numbers.

Suddenly, one of our lot emerged from the station to say they were here – and mobbed up. The Old Bill had gone and it was on big time. They did not expect us to be around and they got an almighty surprise. One copper stood in front of their mob as they poured out of the station and he drew his truncheon and ordered us to keep away, but we were three hundred- to four hundred-handed on all sides. Some of the Under-Fives approached the mob from behind, which also surprised them, and suddenly it was on. They did not know what hit them and they were running in all directions. We chased a mob through the Queens market and ransacked a DIY store, nicking broom handles, dustbin lids etc. We gave them a real going over and we had got one of the best results I have seen at Upton Park.

We knew the Old Bill would be livid after and out in force, so everyone decided to make our way to Aldgate East to await them there. This would be a new tactic, as the police always expected it to go off around the grounds. As my tube arrived at Aldgate there were already about three hundred on the platform and I think they thought we were Leeds. They were about to attack the train and we had to shout that we were West Ham! Fuck that, getting done by this angry lot!

We knew that Leeds would probably be on the next train as there was a long gap before any more trains arrived. People had removed the fire extinguishers and also the spades that accompanied the fire prevention kit on the platform. Suddenly they were here. It was a packed train and they were all jumping up and down singing. The train slowed and before the doors could open the West Ham lot steamed the bloody thing, putting through the windows and trying to get at them before the train had even stopped. We should have waited for the doors to open, but we were too excited. Suddenly police aboard the train were screaming at the driver to carry on and he sped up and out of the station. I knew there would be repercussions and decided to keep a low one and head off, but the others caught the next train and followed Leeds to King's Cross, where by all accounts they had it again. This had been a good day, I reflected. We had had a result before and after and Leeds certainly would remember that visit!

### *THE NORTH-WEST*

It was always exciting to visit Liverpool, Everton, Manchester United or even Manchester City. You knew it could go off anywhere and you had to be on your guard. Two visits stick in my mind from Maine Road during this era. The first time we had a tidy firm and had got away from most of the OB attention and were now deep into Moss Side. The place was very run down, and there was derelict housing and burned-out cars everywhere – and I thought the East End was bad!

We had slipped the OB easily – to be honest, they were pretty clueless in Manchester on most of my visits and this was no exception. Suddenly, though, police arrived from everywhere, and the dog-handlers were well out of order. They told us to all stand still and had us against a wall and were letting the dogs come within an inch of our trousers! We were told that if we didn't stay behind them, and on the pavement, they'd let the dogs go. They were going to escort us to the ground and that was that. But we didn't fancy staying in the away section (which was actually part of the Kippax stand then).

We moved slowly towards the ground, but we noticed that most of the coppers had moved to the front of the escort with only one or two at the back. We decided to stretch the length of the escort by slowing right down, and whilst we had a chance we would break from the middle of the escort unnoticed into a side-street. It was a great plan and worked to perfection. Word went up that the next left was going to be our turning and we were all to leg it as quick as we could to escape the OB at the front and back. Would they notice?

We darted off, about fifty of us, and quickly ran across some gardens and into the back streets and we were away. It was funny at the time – fifty hooligans suddenly running across someone's back garden into a back alley whilst this old dear was hanging out her washing! She couldn't believe what was going on and we were all pissing ourselves laughing. But then were brought back to earth by the sound of sirens screaming all around the place. The OB had realised we were missing and were not impressed. They were on our case and we knew they would be mad.

We chased around the back streets right near the ground, and the locals were astounded to see this mob of geezers escaping the police. We decided to hide in a tiny alleyway and were all stood there puffing away like mad. It seemed like ages, and we were about to move out and go to the ground when a police car appeared at one end of the alley. It drove full speed towards us and I thought to myself, Oh no, here we go … We all stood there transfixed by the fast-approaching car and it screeched to a halt inches from my knees with the two occupants sporting the biggest grins you've ever seen.

But the alley wasn't wide enough for them to open the car doors, as it was only just about wide enough to get the fucking car down it. All of a sudden everyone jumped on to the bonnet, across the roof and down the back and off again. The chase was on. We got close to the ground and mingled with the crowds and we were now free of the OB. We had met up with some of the others from the escort and were now about two hundred-handed. We walked around outside the ground by the Kippax expecting to see them, but nobody was around. So we walked around to the main stand and decided to go in there instead. There were no Mancs around, but we made a noise and let them know we were about in the ground.

At a later game, possibly a Cup game, we played up there midweek. We had hire coaches and were making our way from the coach to the ground but again encountered no resistance, even though we were only fifty or so handed. We entered the ground in the same section as before and then a lot of their boys came in and were sitting in the next section, but we were separated by a fence. I didn't mind Man City and we were sat next to the fence talking to their lot. They even had photos of our firm at Crewe station when we were on the way to Old Trafford once and they were heading somewhere like Stoke. They were pointing out people's faces in our mob and saying they had pictures of them – which was very funny. They seemed sound lads and we had a decent chat. But as the game ended and we all came out it kicked off. There was lots of noise and missiles and people running in all directions but nothing major happened and we made our way home.

I also had a lot of time for the Scousers, although they could be nasty buggers when you were there for the football. They loved their Stanley knives and you could come unstuck if you weren't careful up there. But I had mates there and often would go for the weekend and have a real crack.

One night we had drawn Liverpool in the League Cup at Anfield and we hired a number of coaches (you couldn't get home from Liverpool by train midweek unless you left by about 9pm!). We had lost the other two coaches as we had the short straw and got an old banger of a coach. It parked up next to Stanley Park and about forty of us went to look for the others. We thought they'd be in a boozer somewhere so we tried the Blue House next to Everton's ground, which was just down the road. They weren't about, but there were a few Liverpool lads in there playing pool. We grabbed a quick beer but it kicked off inside ten minutes and our lot were chasing the Scousers out the pub and up the road.

We left, about ten of us, and made our way through the very dark Stanley Park towards Anfield. We got to the ground and then saw the rest of our boys from the other coaches. We all went in the Anfield Road End, but in the home section rather than the away part. It was a classic game and we were beaten (2-1, I think). We left the ground just before the final whistle and we were well handy. Two hundred top boys, all the old faces, and looking for Scousers. We found them all right!

It was mayhem in the back streets as we chased after them, giving them a right old hiding. It seemed to last for ages as we ran them several times. We gave a good account of ourselves that night, and some of my Liverpool friends told me later how impressed they were with West Ham that night. One of them told me he was 'threatened by this huge black bloke' who picked him up by the throat and held him off his feet against a wall. The OB were not very happy with our lot that night, and it was around 11pm before we eventually got back to our coaches near the ground. A late night, that one ...

Manchester United were always a force, no matter what anyone says. When you can come across a mob of about a thousand it certainly sobers you up quickly. We had many battles with the Reds, some of which I will recall here. My favourite was the FA Cup game up at Old Trafford when we took about eight thousand up there. As mentioned before, the OB were not the brightest force and we had a plan that, when the train pulled into Piccadilly, we would make our way over to the right-hand side, away from the main entrance, and through the back way.

There were a load of OB by the platform as the train pulled in and they had lined up loads of buses outside the station. But we were having none of it. Some on our train wanted the buses and so the OB were confused as we split in two directions. We calmly walked over to the rear entrance and were suddenly out in the streets. People were too excited, understandably, and we were a chasing pack on the move and well pumped up! I don't know what went wrong but suddenly while talking to one of my mates I realised we were down to about ten of us! The others had taken a turning, we hadn't been watching and were suddenly alone. There were two of us and five or six other guys that we never knew, some of whom had colours on!

We decided to make our way back to the main road and

then back towards Piccadilly where we would get our bearings together before setting off again. We walked around a few back streets and heard a big off in the distance. The usual noise and smashing glasses. We were gutted that we were missing out on the action but we were definitely headed in the right direction. We turned a few corners and all of a sudden the main road was in front of us. We turned into this main road, which I knew led back to the station, and we were suddenly in front of about a hundred or so blokes outside a boozer. We didn't know who they were, but we couldn't turn back. As we neared it was obvious they were Mancs, some of them were nursing sore heads and one or two had cuts. They had just met the famous ICF!

We muttered under our breath to each other that the best plan would be to front it and walk straight through them without too much fuss. We had our heads down but before we even reached them I heard a northern voice shout, 'Look, they're West Ham, let's have 'em.' With that, the whole lot of them ran towards us and I half shut my eyes expecting the first whack on the head. But they ran straight past the two of us and into the stragglers behind us up the road with their colours on! There *is* a God.

We made it to the station and then met up with the rest of the firm in a pub. We had a good turn-out here, but they had the numbers. They knew where we were but they didn't manage to get into us at all. We went into the ground and about fifty to sixty of us were in the seats to the right of the main West Ham support above the Paddock, which housed all the mouthy Mancs. There was loads of abuse between the away end and the Paddock, with missiles flying everywhere. We were well beaten in the game and five minutes away from the end we decided to get up and make an exit. The Mancs below spotted us and started singing,

'We can see you sneaking out', the cheeky gits. But we got outside and found the entrance to the Paddock was open to allow fans to get out.

We psyched ourselves and each other up and decided to make a go of it in there. Run in, catch them by surprise, throw a few punches and cause a big opening and then get out. It worked a treat, we entered into their Paddock and sent them running – they were unaware that we were only fifty or so handed. They came back at us, but we weren't in the mood for running. It was a good toe-to-toe for about five minutes before we turned and got out, only to re-enter at the next entrance along the stand! We could hear the West Ham end going crazy – shouts of 'IiiiiiiiiiCeeeeeeeEfffffff' rang out.

After the game there were thousands of the fuckers all over the place and another mate of mine took a right old blow to the head from an umbrella. But we had got a result as far as we were concerned and we reassured ourselves on the train home that not many teams would ever do that at Old Trafford. Even less would try it at Upton Park, in our eyes.

Another year at OT, they tried to ambush our train at Piccadilly but we were having none of it and gave them some back. After the game, we were making our way back on the branch line when they again tried to ambush our train. But we jumped off and tried to get at them up the steps from the platform before the OB restored order. The Mancs always brought a good firm to Upton Park and one year we had heard from a Cockney Red that they were planning to get out at Plaistow. They were to cause a bit of trouble a couple of miles from the ground, and think they had got a result away from the main mob of West Ham. But we caught wind of this and we had packed out the Victoria and Lord Stanley pubs waiting for them. They got the surprise of their lives that night as we met them full on!

## THE STRANGEST THINGS

There were many occasions where we headed for games not expecting much to happen, only to be caught up in widespread violence. One particular place was Lincoln for a night match at Sincil Bank. We had caught the train up and made our way to the game for a midweek League Cup tie. At the ground, some of the boys were turning up with lumps on their head saying they had encountered a sizeable mob, all casual, and got a bit of a hiding. We hadn't expected this and thought maybe another firm from nearby was using the occasion to have a go at us – although I don't know who they were, or if this was true.

We decided to leave the game early. Most of the other lads had travelled up in coaches, so we didn't know what to do. Should we roam the streets with them to try and hunt this so-called mob? If we did, we could end up by the coaches and have to make our own way back to the station in the opposite direction! Or did we want to risk going straight to the station and miss all the action?

In the end we followed the main group and looked for Lincoln everywhere after the game, but alas they weren't about. There were a few minor skirmishes, and I must admit I saw two of their lot walk straight into our mob from a side street. Someone fronted them and asked if they wanted it – one to one and nobody else would join in. One of them only accepted, but I bet he wished he hadn't! The guy who hit him only took one punch and left him counting the chickens flying around his head ... he was out cold. We never did find their boys and to this day I don't know what all the earlier action had been about.

We also played Wigan in a home Cup tie and they brought about two thousand down. Nobody was expecting action and so we were all drinking in our favourite pubs rather than mobbing up around the station. I hear that their mob came out and took liberties with the few people who were around. We went after them following the game, as we heard they had a special train leaving from Barking station. We caught a little group of them outside the station that night and took revenge, but all in all it was hard to get at them because of OB presence in and around the station.

I've seen it kick off on my travels to such places as Grimsby, Bury, Bolton and Brighton and you could never predict some of these events. I don't think much of Nottingham Forest, but one year we went up there and they were particularly gobby outside. We sat in the nice new stand to the left of the Trent End on a very cold and misty Saturday afternoon. We left, as usual, five minutes before the end and walked behind their end looking for them. We crossed the bridge and suddenly I saw some of the Under-Fives steam into a small group of blokes who were obviously not up for it and were normal supporters. But one of the lads struck one of these Forest blokes with a blade across his face and down his throat and his whole face opened up. This was out of order for me, as the guy obviously didn't warrant it and was protesting his innocence when he was cut. We walked around a bit and then found their boys near the station. We ran them ragged and chased them into the bus station nearby. Near the station was a car park leading into what looked like a shopping centre. We marched through there and I was hoping for some action as these tossers had pissed me off today.

We didn't find them but instead stumbled across some really lippy local black lads who were skating or skateboarding through this car park. They were game and mouthed off so we hit them real hard. They probably don't know to this day who they had just encountered as they were nothing to do with the football, but they called it and for their troubles they got it.

Birmingham was always another good place where you knew it would blow. The FA Cup game against them in the Eighties was legendary. They stuffed us on the pitch so we stuffed them inside the ground and the match was twice abandoned as we ran across the pitch into their end. It was mayhem that day, and everyone seemed to lose their cool at the same time. People were smashing up cars and all sorts outside the ground. I saw one lot take a police motorcyclist out and it was kicking off all the way back to the station.

I had strayed from the main group (again!) and was making my way with two mates right through the middle of the Bullring when we entered a shop for some fags and food for the train journey home. There were loads of big black guys everywhere – not the football type, they were just hanging. One of them came up to me in the shop and very quietly whispered in my ear (in a strange Jamaican/ Brummie accent) that if he ever saw me around there again he'd have me. I turned to look at him, ready to clock him one, and as I turned he was facing me with a huge toothless grin and slowly brought a large carving knife up and out of his trousers to show me! It had to be around two foot long and I was in no mood to argue with the fucker. I quickly made my way out of the shop and down to the station below us.

Wolves had a little dig at us following one game up there after we sat separately from the main away support in the only new stand that was built at that stage. But we chased them through the car parks after they launched a flurry of rocks and stones on us at the ground. We walked right round the ground and had a few offs but some of our lot said they were ambushed under the subway after the game.

I'm sure there are loads of supporters out there shouting, 'Why hasn't he mentioned this row, or that row, or when we done this or that' and I'm sure a lot of the stories are valid. But time has fazed my memory and most of this collection of stories stand out most vividly in my memory. I don't believe it will ever be the same again, as all-seater stadiums, CCTV and increased police awareness have put the authorities one step ahead of the hooligan. In my time, we were at least two steps ahead of the OB and everything they did was reactive rather than proactive. I still go to West Ham today, as do lots of boys from this era, but nothing is ever organised and people want to keep their heads down and get on with their lives without the threat of newspaper exposures and police harassment.

I wouldn't like to comment on who are, or aren't, the present-day guvnors and I'm sure everyone has their own opinion. I can't be arsed with the stupid comments you get on some of the hooligan websites, although Darren's 'In The Know' site doesn't have as many idiots as some of the others attract. When people start talking about 'we had twenty-five boys' it makes me chuckle. They would have pissed their pants if they had ever encountered the Red Army on a big day – or the ICF, for that matter.

## CHAPTER EIGHT
# THE BANNING ORDER

One West Ham lad wrote to me and told a bit of his story about the banning order he received – this is what he had to say:

*I suppose I have always taken an interest in the aggro at football, since I was a boy. I always loved seeing it go off, loved the atmosphere, the going mental at goals and the general banter between the two sets of fans.*

*I have always followed West Ham, but because of my family ties up north I followed Sunderland and York City and saw them almost as often as I did the Hammers.*

*Looking back, I had some great times watching football and trouble all over the country, even going to the odd Yid, Gooner and Chelsea games with my school mates. In fact, if there was an aggro game on, more often than not we would try and be there, even if it meant only going down to Euston or somewhere to suss out the scene.*

*Every Saturday was the same – wherever you were*

travelling. We would be looking at the fixtures in the papers and saying, 'Pompey v Leeds, it will go off there deffo, 657 and Service Crew are top firms,' or 'Bristol City v Tranmere? – yeah could go there, both little tasty firms them. A mate of mine took a slap at Ashton Gate once.' All that sort of shit as well as what stations mobs would have to change etc. (New St at Birmingham was a great one for this).

I went to school in north London in a fairly hard area where fighting was always on the menu. Ironically I was probably a bit of a wanker at school compared to the other casual and football lads and this probably drew me to the firms and the offs all the more. I felt accepted and part of things far more than I ever did on my own manor.

Over the years I copped plenty of slaps, been taxed for clothes and run by mobs. I still loved it and to be fair I have seen plenty of blinding rows and doled out plenty of sly little digs and boots myself and got the buzz from running other mobs and arriving en masse in some other town or area and noising the place up.

By about the 1986/87 season (the season after our great third- place finish) I had left school, had more dough and got to know several other like-minded north London lads who followed West Ham and from there the fun really started as we joined in with a little crew from Bow and became what could be described as a bit of an ICF fan club.

There we would be trying to get involved on the edges wherever we could, spotting, looking out for wherever the older lads were going to be. I know it sounds a bit sad now but at the time the ICF had *a blinding name and I suppose we basked in the reflected glory.*

*Things chugged on nicely for a couple of years like this, with us gradually getting more involved without realising it. We were still young lads, fairly small and unnoticed as a rule and things were definitely tasty in terms of the rows we had.*

*1988/89 was an absolutely shit season on the pitch for us. To be honest, apart from the amazing record in both Cups and an incredible late season rally we were heading for the drop almost from the off. Opening the season at Southampton with a 4-0 trouncing and losing to bloody Charlton at home in our first home game pointed the way it was likely to read.*

*Things were very different off the pitch though, with us taking thousands away and getting involved in at least one incident every week.*

*The Acid House scene was taking off and there was tons of talk about it, but most of the lads were still into the football and casual thing and most of us had not done our first 'E' yet!*

*Arsenal at home in the League that year was a particularly memorable one, with their mob being ambushed by us at Plaistow after the game (which, predictably, we lost). It was amazing, the Old Bill did not seem to have got wind of it and it went on at every stop until we were finally booted off at Mile End. During the mayhem one of our lot got cut with a Stanley across the arm and at one point one of the Gooners had it up down the tracks, it was that fierce.*

*A few weeks later there was the legendary game at Millwall that received all the publicity on the*

Transport Police documentary. For some reason lost in the mists of time most of our little crew weren't there that day. I know it certainly was not for lack of wanting to be there. Even in my reformed state I do regret not having been there to experience it.

The season marched on towards Christmas with a few more high-profile games, including a couple against Liverpool, the first of which was in the League where it went off at the Queens market. Then my mates and I nearly got ambushed at Whitechapel and then there was the famous 4-1 Hammers win in the Littlewoods Cup where we did not see much go on off the pitch but the game itself will live long in the memory.

After a January that included a famous Cup replay win at Highbury we faced our old nemesis the Mancs at Upton Park in what for me was to be a very memorable and, looking back, life-changing game. A mate of mine from York had come down for the weekend and although he was a loyal Manc who regularly travelled to Old Trafford he knew the score and was willing to experience the other side of the fence and keep his head down with us.

We got down to Upton Park at about 1.30 and went straight into the Queens to see who was about and if anything had occurred earlier. Nothing much had, the usual rumours were going about but little more. After a couple of jars we headed over the square to Charleens (at that time a particularly lively bar), to see if we could sit tight and quiet and pick up any hints about where things were going to go off. It's no exaggeration to say that my northern mate's guts were going nineteen to the dozen at that point!

At 2.45, with no visible action about to happen and tons of Old Bill making themselves busy, we decided to make a move into the ground to get a decent spot on the South Bank. Once at the ground it became apparent that United had brought a better than usual following and that we were going to be penned right in to the final section of the South Bank by the 'Chicken Run'. This fact had stoked an already volatile atmosphere and the place was pumping by the time the teams ran out.

Although I don't remember the score that day (it could've been 3-1 to them), I know United pretty much played us off the park and that throughout the game the main focus was on the atmosphere between the two sets of supporters. For some strange reason the Old Bill stood back and let all manner of abuse fly around (they normally ejected or nicked you for next to nothing in there!).

Coming out of the ground we headed straight back to the Queens for a quick pint before jumping over to Charleens to wait for the United escort to come past. The atmosphere in Charleens was throbbing. It was packed to the rafters and a DJ was playing House on the decks. The windows were steamed but you could make out police horses and dogs with their handlers blocking off the square as the first of the United escort came up Green Street.

The back service doors leading out of the rear of the Queens market were opened and the bar emptied out into the loading bays and headed for the side road that runs into Green Street. The mob must have been two hundred-strong and we all steamed straight up at the shocked Mancs and Old Bill.

The scene was mayhem – bottles and glass flew, figures pelted past and the usual roar went up. It went mad for about a minute before lots of people who started first began backing off and then running. Being at the back a few of us thought it was the Mancs and stood, before realising the Old Bill had let the dogs off of their leads and were charging us.

Too late I bolted and headed back up to Charleens. There was a bottleneck of lads trying to get in and a dog got me by the ankle and yanked me back. Next thing I knew I was on my stomach with another dog on my elbow while the first dog kept gnawing at my ankle (I still have the scars).

Two Old Bill came up and joined in the fun. One booted me in the ribs and the other truncheoned me between the shoulder blades. One of the wags says, 'Don't move.' They call the dogs off and I am led around into Green Street by two coppers and lobbed into the back of a van. I am wearing a white Peter Werth jumper and the fucking thing looks well weighed in by now. I am shaken and starting to realise I'm in the shit. This isn't some silly ground ejection or being led around the pitch.

A few more lads are bundled in and we are taken to West Ham control under the West Stand, almost an Old Bill station in its own right. We end up being taken down to [name withheld], a juvenile court at the arse end of the docklands as Plaistow was full of Manc scum and East Ham was full of our lot.

After being printed, photo taken etc., I finally get let out in time to get back to meet my mates and have a quick pint before closing time.

Ten days later I am up at the Magistrates Court

charged with threatening behaviour. The duty solicitor advises me to plead guilty. He says my case is mitigated by the fact it's a first offence and all that kind of crap. I feel well pissed off, I want to get this over as quickly as possible.

After a half a day of listening to the sometimes amusing litany of cases being prosecuted from the game – 'The defendant was heard to sing songs relating to the Munich air disaster and seen to make aeroplane- type motions'; 'The defendant was heard to say, "You Manc c\*\*ts are going to get it after"' – I am then called up.

The charge of threatening and using violent behaviour is read out and I plead guilty. The next thing I know the prosecution barrister rises and says, 'The defendant was seen to advance, throw a bottle and decamp the scene.' Fucking Old Bill! This is all new to me, but it is too late now, I have pleaded. The magistrates huddle for a minute and make a decision – they find me guilty. They burble on about the bottle throwing (non-existent) and the gravity of the offence. I am given a £500 fine, have to pay court costs and worst of all receive a year's ban from all Football League grounds in England (an exclusion order).

Now I know I can't really grumble as I was there and had intent, but I always felt I had been shafted a bit. One thing for certain, it changed the path of my life. I got into the burgeoning rave scene and eventually at the end of summer '89 I met the woman who is now my wife and best mate. I am still a casual and still get a rush watching any little incidents that go off and enjoy hearing the tales of the current lads, *but for me that January day in 1989 was the end of the road hoolie-wise. There is simply too much to lose, the odds are stacked against what are perceived as public enemies and folk devils.*

# CHAPTER NINE

# ARSENAL (THE GOONERS)

If there was ever a London team that had a large following but do not get much recognition it is the Arsenal. We have all heard how they have been called the invisible mob by some. In fact, quite a few times I have seen them disappear from their end without being noticed. This is not to say they are a waste of time as a firm. Their relationship with their most hated rivals, the Tottenham Hotspurs, is one of bitter rivalry and, when the two sets of fans meet, it can be guaranteed there will be trouble between the two.

Spurs, commonly known as the Yids (by themselves and most other sides), have a large following and many old fans, and even the new ones still believe in the glory days of the Sixties. In fact, apart from the odd Cup win they have done fuck all since those days when they dominated the football scene. The first English club to do the double, they were quick to take the piss out of their north London rivals, but it wasn't long before the tables turned and Arsenal were the force in north London, if not the whole of London. Only recently Chelsea sides have had a bit of success and, let's face it, Chelsea are the Man United of the south. At least Arsenal can say they have more than one Englishman in the side, although the French connection at Arsenal is slowly taking over.

The trouble with Arsenal fans is they expect success every year, and when it doesn't come they are the first to whine, something their manager seems to have grasped quite well. If ever a team (apart from Man United) had loads of glory-hunting fans it is Arsenal. The 'real' fan hates this new breed of followers, but in the club's eyes it is arses on seats and all money in the bank.

The new fans have no idea what it was like at football before the all-seater, and sit safely tucked up in the North Bank, along with thousands of other fellow fans, sitting safely behind the stewards and giving it the large one at rival supporters, knowing they can't be touched.

Arsenal are not alone in these stakes and other London clubs, Chelsea for one, are much the same. The only difference is that the Chelsea boys always looked to Old Bill to hide behind, then started giving it the large one. Fair play to Chelsea – they have had some top lads who did not give a fuck, but as always the hangers-on fucked it for them.

I have been to a few Arsenal games (where they were not playing West Ham) and I was surprised at their fans – totally different lot. I could not believe the change and wondered if I was at the same ground. I went to a north London derby at White Hart Lane (or 'Three-Point Lane' as we call it) and I saw some of the best fighting I had ever seen – or worst, depending on where you stand on the issue. To say they hated each other would be an understatement. The Paxton was a bloodbath and outside Old Bill had no control whatsoever. Both set of fans steamed into each other without regard for what was going on around them. I could not believe the change in attitude and wondered why they weren't like this when they played us.

To say Arsenal are a top firm would be stretching the truth, but all the same they are a handy one. In all fairness, if they took a drop down a division for a season or two it would clean out all the hangers-on. Arsenal always had a large Irish following as many a Paddy played for them, and they were nicknamed the London Irish by many. Now days it seems the London French is more apt. I know many a lifelong Arsenal fan who reckons if the side goes the way of Chelsea and ends up mainly all French they would give them away and follow their local side in a lower league and only turn out now and again for big games, mainly for a chance of a bit of action.

I have been involved with the Gooner fans on the terraces first-hand, and I am glad I was West Ham and not one of them, although they are not to be taken lightly. I have copped a bit of a kicking from their fans on the tube and I do not take them for granted.

A few stories lads have sent me back up what I say but the big one for Arsenal fans was in the UEFA Cup final of 2000. The eyes of the real fans throughout the world, England especially, were on them. They played the Turkish side Galatasaray, who in previous rounds had caused a fair bit of trouble. This was overlooked by UEFA, and even the death of two Leeds fans who were stabbed by Gala fans was dismissed by football officials as only thugs attacking innocent Turks. The fact is, two fans died, and no one did fuck all about it. English fans called for revenge and, when Arsenal played the Turks in the final, the eyes of the football world were on them – not on the Turks, who were made out to be the innocent victims.

Cries from rival gangs of an England united against the Turks in Copenhagen went out and the press as usual beat the story up in the papers. Police concerns that a large English army of football hooligans was going to descend on

Europe were unfounded. There was trouble at the game and as usual the Turks legged it. The day was Arsenal's. They kicked them all over Copenhagen and only the odd straggler Arsenal scarfer got set upon by the cowardly Turks, most carrying knives. They were clearly seen on TV as being provoked by the Turks and the Arsenal lads settled a few scores. The press did not mention if they were the lads attacked, but branded them as thugs, even digging up the past history of one fan who was stabbed and labelling him a troublemaker. As the saying with the press goes, 'never let the truth get in the way of a good story.'

Most Arsenal fans that day were well pissed off at losing the game, let alone a final. To have Turks taking the piss is one thing, but giving the odd lone fan a kicking was well out of order as far as the Gooners were concerned. 'Welcome to hell' is the Gala catchphrase. Well, it seemed hell was going to get dowsed a fair bit to show the Turks what cowards they are.

Calls came out from officials of UEFA saying it could ruin England's chance of hosting the World Cup if there was trouble. What annoys me is this – why were Gala there in the first place? They should have been thrown out after the death of the Leeds fans, or at least played the game in England and had their fans barred from attending.

If the truth be known, the majority of Arsenal lads did not want trouble. It came when the Turks provoked them and they stood their ground – and good on them. The press and Home Office officials labelled them troublemakers. That makes me laugh. I know, if someone had a go at me with a knife or a chair, I would do what I could to defend myself. Rather be 'tried by twelve than carried by six' any day.

A few things that came out of that game made me laugh. A look around the hooligan boards revealed that all sorts of claims were being made. The one I liked best was that a Chelsea lad was spotted on TV and so there must have been some Headhunters there and they had the day. It came from a lad who goes to both Chelsea and Arsenal, but is mainly a Gooner. The Rent Boys were quick to try and claim the glory – strange that, not like them!

The day was the Gooners'. There may have been a few other fans from other clubs there, but they did not claim it and all the credit goes to the Gooners: well done, Arsenal. You weren't an invisible mob this time.

In Europe, English fans always have had a bad name, but never Arsenal, and to see the Arsenal fans have a go back at the Turks shocked many. Again UEFA blamed the English, ignoring the stabbing of an Arsenal fan and the deaths of the two Leeds fans. In fact, the press went into overdrive, digging up as much dirt as they could on the stabbed Arsenal fan after he was discharged from hospital. He was given the VIP treatment in a director's box at Copenhagen. The press, however, claimed he had been imprisoned for hooliganism in the past. Does this mean getting a blade in the back by Turks fans was a just reward and the Turks were justified in their actions? UEFA seems to think it was OK. Had it been the other way round I bet Leeds would have played their return leg behind closed doors.

Some Arsenal lads, in fact, nearly all, were just looking for a quiet bar to have a drink and stay away from the many Turks around the town. One lad said he was in a bar with his mates and the police parked up their riot vans outside. This in turn attracted the Turks to them. While no trouble went off, a lot of slagging went on and made things a bit uneasy. In one bar about a hundred Arsenal fans started singing and the Turks thought there were thousands of them and they all ran and got help. Many came back with knives, axes etc. The police did not seem interested, and of course the press were there. Had that been in England the police would have cleared the streets of opposing fans and minimised the trouble, but not the Danish Police.

Many lads left the bar in smaller groups to go back to their hotels and were set upon by roaming groups of Turkish fans in alleyways. The Arsenal lads held their own and the Turks, who did not think the English would stand, were shaken and most legged it. One lad told me many had knives and he was surprised that there were not more stabbings. He reckons it was scary but there was no way he and his mates were bottling to the Turks, and they knew the next day would be worse. The worst part was losing the Cup to them.

Some other stories I have been told about Arsenal show that they are not to be taken lightly, although, being a West Ham fan, we never did expect much from them and were right in most cases. One lad wrote to me and said he was at the Arsenal tube when the train pulled in and a load of lads said, 'West Ham only in here.' He got on with his mate and they were all Gooners – the two of them copped a fair kicking and were thrown off the next station.

The story I liked best was the 1980 FA Cup final when West Ham were in the old Second Division and Arsenal were favourites to win the Cup. Talk had it we would have no support because we were down a league. Nothing could have been further from the truth. Many a sleeping Hammers fan turned out and the Gooners did not want to know. That was the only West Ham final I have missed (except the 'white horse' one) and from what I have been told it was a right piss-take.

A couple of times West Ham have met the Arsenal, after my time and when I was already in Australia. One incident, which led to the fatal stabbing of an Arsenal fan on May 2, was recalled by a West Ham lad who was on the tube coming back from the game:

> *Micky, it happened in the long tunnels beneath Arsenal tube station. Arsenal were in wait, ready to ambush us, we had sixty to seventy West Ham on it. There were hundreds of the fuckers on the platforms when the train pulled in (this was some time after the game and after it had gone off all over the place in the streets of Highbury).*
>
> *As the train pulled in a huge roar went up from their mob and they began battering the train. As the doors opened they expected to jump on and batter West Ham, but they didn't anticipate that these were game boys!*
>
> *West Ham actually jumped off the train and steamed into them and chased them back through those long tunnels. It was then that the Arsenal lad was stabbed and killed. From what I heard he pulled a blade out and it backfired on him. That Arsenal mob had all sorts of weapons that day and we relieved a few from them. Many were dropped as they legged it. I have never seen an Arsenal mob like it before, with us all tooled up as well. I used to take them lightly, but never again.*

A Gooner fan who was with that mob tells me it was different. He reckons the West Ham lads had more like five hundred. His version is much the same except he never saw the stabbing, but confirmed that the Arsenal lads were all tooled up:

> *The fucking Hammers were all over the place. Just as you thought you had found one mob, another would*

come along and link up. They were mental and it was on for ages after the game. Loads of us headed to the tube and reckoned most had gone by now. We waited for the train to come in and it was loaded with Hammers, fuck, we never stood a chance. They jumped off and in to us. My arse was going, I tell you. Our lads were copping a kicking and I got away. I had a bottle which I dropped, and legged it. I have never seen a mob so mental. Loads of our lads pissed off to the outside of the station. You could hear the roar all the way up to the road, then it went all quiet. Old Bill turned up and I decided it was safe to go back down. Most had gone by now and I had my scarf well hidden. I had heard stories about West Ham not wearing colours and I found out first-hand that day. I was lucky I got away as more and more Old Bill came to the station.

Rumours were going round that a lad had been thrown on the tracks, so I never went back down the tube; instead I got a bus. It was later I found out the Arsenal lad was stabbed. I tell you what, I have never been so scared in my life as I was that day. Talks were the Arsenal lad pulled a blade on a Hammer and had it turned around on him. I dunno if that's true but I do know I never wore colours again when we played West Ham, even some seventeen to eighteen years after.

I have seen some offs in my time, but that day was mental. When we play West Ham even now, I keep thinking they are all over. You don't see them till it's too late and going down to Upton Park is itself a fucking scary place. The only time you see a white face is on game day and walking from the station down to the ground must be one of the worst going. Even if the

*ground is a shithole, I am glad when I get inside. One
year I took my motor and I had an Arsenal car sticker
on it. After the game I had death threats all over my
windscreen. I reckon I was lucky as I found out many
had their tyres slashed and the paintwork done in.
West Ham – fuck them, you can have them.*

Judging by what he says, he doesn't like West Ham! He
admits going tooled up even if it was only a bottle. If he
wasn't going to use it, then why take it? Same as the knife
scenario – if you carry a blade, in my eyes, you pull it, you
have to use it. God help you if you are bluffing. I dunno if the
Arsenal lad was bluffing, but he paid the ultimate price.

Another West Ham lad tells of his experiences with the
Gooners:

*My first visit to Arsenal's ground was sometime in
February 1977. Word had gone around Upton Park
that we always took over the place and we all thought
we had a God-given right just to turn up and claim the
North Bank. Five of us travelled to north London and
joined up with about twenty others at Holborn. We
walked into the North Bank in ones and twos and
made our way to the top of the terrace. All around
Gooners were looking nervy. West Ham were all over
the place in their beloved North Bank.*

*Word was spreading around: 'West Ham's in here.'
It did not take much longer before a decent-sized West
Ham mob had got together. A little burst of 'Bubbles',
together with the fear already in the North Bank
regulars, sent the fuckers scattering all over the place.
Roars of approval came from the Clock End – West
Ham had taken it again. A small Gooner mob had a*

*go back but it did not last long as we were beaten back by Old Bill, who were making a better attempt at getting it back for them. Arsenal went one up early, which caused a few surges into them. West Ham amazingly went 2-1 in front near half-time. Arsenal had a go back, but we stayed in there till the end and half the North Bank seemed to be celebrating a fine 3-2 win at the end.*

### *NEXT SEASON, OCTOBER 1977*

*We got to the ground at around 12.30 and we scouted around for a while. Old Bill were trying to get us on the Clock End. We kept moving on and I met up with a mate of mine whose nose had been splattered all over his face. Him and three other boys had been at Holborn when a train pulled in full of a mob of lads. The doors opened and one bloke shouted, 'West Ham, only West Ham boys on here.' Not suspecting anything the boys jumped on the train and the doors closed. It was a carriage full of Gooners and they got a right mullering – a painful lesson learned.*

*We got in to the North Bank from the right-hand side thirty-handed and announced our arrival and immediately got stampeded by Gooners. We were well outnumbered and I for one was expecting a right kicking. But the Arsenal boys weren't interested – they were already on the run from a West Ham mob already doing their thing. We had the North Bank again, but our little mob had been sussed. The only thing for us to do was get amongst our lot in the middle.*

*Loads of little offs as we tried to get in the centre. Old Bill attacked the main West Ham lot and a large Gooner mob had a go from the far side of the North*

Bank. The battle ebbed and flowed. A big Gooner c\*\*t was using the plaster cast of his broken arm well, sending loads of lads flying. He was finally brought down under a flurry of boots. We certainly weren't having our own way this time.

Strictly speaking, I don't know if we took it or not but we certainly caused loads of mayhem. There was a massive ruck, about two hundred a side outside the tube station. Bottles and bricks thrown everywhere and Old Bill steaming in, nicking right, left and centre and the animal with a c\*\*t halfway up its back (a police horse) had its c\*\*t removed by a breeze block to the approval of both mobs.

Moments later the Gooners had enough and ran off down some side roads. The Old Bill moved us into the station and on to the train. Two stops later the train was smashed to fuck as we went fucking mental (God knows why). The train stayed in the tunnel for 45 minutes then it crawled into a station. We got a few slaps off Old Bill and some got nicked and it took ages to get home. All this on top of a 3-0 defeat.

Next season Arsenal at home. The Gooners were down Green Street in threes and fours; there was plenty of slaps being handed out near the Queens.

Inside, Arsenal were in the South Bank and by half-time the mood was very anti-Arsenal. They were 2-0 up, one of them a disputed goal by MacDonald whose enjoyment of the moment was cut short when an uninvited guest ran on to the pitch from the 'Chicken Run' and tried to remove his head from his shoulders.

A few Gooners not in the South Bank were getting turned over by blokes as old as sixty, it seemed, who were dishing it out in the seats. I was later told by a Gooner who was in the South Bank that most of them did not think they would make it home in one piece and have never been so scared before or since.

The atmosphere was well sinister. A last-minute goal got us a 2-2 draw and you could sense the relief in the away bit of the South Bank and Arsenal colours that had not been lifted were hidden as they made their way to the station.

### 1980 FA CUP FINAL

The day started in Barking at 9.00am, taking the piss out of a mate who had a broken jaw from the night before at a club in Basildon. We weren't expecting too much of a ruck at the final. It did not seem like a normal game – for one thing, everyone had their colours on. We weren't expected to win so everyone seemed up for enjoying a crack and getting behind the team. Having said that, we would be going through north London, so there was every chance of an off in the tube.

The day was a mass of claret and blue. It was a case of 'spot the Gooner' down Wembley way. I saw no trouble, just the odd slap, but, if Arsenal wanted it, they would have been killed.

As you well know, Micky, we won. Afterwards it was a gigantic piss-take of the Gooners and the only plans being made was to go on the piss, but fuck knows what would have happened if we'd lost. The Gooners kept on saying the FA Cup final did not matter as they had a European final some four days later.

The night of their Euro final and we were on the piss still. In my local, the Acorn, a massive roar lifted the roof as the Gooner player put a penalty over the bar and the Gooners tasted defeat again.

### 1982 AWAY

The Old Bill were everywhere. A few little offs in the side street, which we won well. We split up and got into the North Bank in dribs and drabs. The ICF were in there and a few minor scuffles broke out before the main event, which took place half an hour or so before the 3pm kick-off.

A load of us got behind their boys and the feared ICF roar went up. A smoke bomb went off and it was complete mayhem. Loads of them escaped on to the pitch. I took a few digs and gave a few out.

This was the time of the Falklands war and with the smoke bomb going off it seemed pretty apt we sustained casualties. I would like to say, 'I counted us all in and all back again' (Max Hastings on HMS Hermes, I think), but I can't because a few of our lot were unconscious and a load more had their collars felt.

Arsenal had a few more and regained ground. I read in a C*l*n W*r* book that they feel they had a result that day, but, as ever, we had to take it to them. It got nasty outside as a mob of Gooners had a pop at us as we left the ground. The Old Bill were on the scene quickly but we won the battle and a few more of us spent an evening in the company of the boys in blue. For the record a Gooner was stabbed outside the ground. He was knifed during an off.

Nothing much since. We went into the North Bank next season, again in dribs and drabs, but we did not seem to get it together and did not have the numbers.

*It was proving difficult to get on the North Bank as Old Bill were well on the case – maybe as a result of the knifing the year before.*

*A mob of Gooners had a pop on the forecourt, mainly a few kids, autograph hunters etc., but at least they made an attempt. Other than that I have seen nothing and stopped going on a regular basis in the early Nineties, having a wife and kids and lack of funds, so I am well out of touch. As with our London neighbours, we lost a few but won many, almost always in enemy territory.*

The Gooners seem to be getting it together and a few years ago gave the Mancs a going over at Highbury – nothing major, but they done some small mobs and run the rest. Again it was reported the Mancs met up well away from the ground before being sussed out and, what do you know, the Old Bill turned up as soon as some Gooners found them! Sound familiar? There were 150-odd lads and they were escorted to the ground under the watchful eyes of the Gooner fans. The usual 'I'm safe behind Old Bill' slagging began by the Mancs. A mob of about two hundred Arsenal tried having a pop at them but the Old Bill were thick on the ground and kept the fans apart. The Old Bill cameramen made many think twice, as they were filming most lads. The game over and the Mancs winning 2-1, the Gooners went looking for some blood.

A large mob agreed to meet up at the Drayton Park pub, only to find a mob of about one hundred-odd Mancs there before them. Some Gooner stragglers copped a slap, a few got a bit of a kicking and the Mancs claimed a result. They were too early in their celebrations – they never noticed about a hundred and fifty to two hundred Gooner lads coming down the road. Once again the Old Bill were called on for escort and the Gooner lads were held back with a blockade across the road with vans and Old Bill keeping an eye on things. Some of the Gooners headed towards Holloway tube station and came across a mob of some forty-odd Mancs, who saw the size of the mob coming at them and legged it.

Some ran into the tube. The Old Bill at the station sussed out what was going on and closed the gates, keeping the main mob out, but some got in before they closed and had a field day with the Mancs. It was reported that a few Cockney Reds hid their scarves and claimed to be Arsenal fans. It never worked – they copped a slap for their trouble, the rest got a good kicking. Many cried out for the Old Bill to escort them back to Euston, where many other Mancs were – they looked like they had been through a war zone.

Their so-called victory was short lived. The Gooners had turned them over well – in fact, if Old Bill had not sussed out the lads when they did there would have been more copping it. So much for the Cockney Reds. All mouth again and when they know they are going to cop a kicking, and there is no way out, why not have a go? When you are asked the time by someone and your accent gives you away, and you can get away with it, is one thing. Being sussed out and knowing you are about to receive a slap, why bother crying wolf? I reckon the boots would have gone in harder, just for being a Judas. Then again, most of them are part-timers who only follow a winning side and a few years ago no doubt were cheering on the Arsenal when they did the double.

# CHAPTER TEN

# EURO 2000 AND THE WORLD CUP

If there was ever a football competition that attracted attention from the fans, media and government bodies all over Europe it was Euro 2000. England had qualified by beating the Scots in a two-match affair, winning at Hampden 2-0 then losing at Wembley 1-0. This was seen by many fans as a warm-up for Euro 2000.

The trouble between rival fans in Scotland and the return leg in Wembley, where the blame was laid solely on England supporters, was the start of a slow fuse leading up to the main competition. England fans were branded hooligans in London because they fought the Scots and according to most reports, to quote a Jock song, 'sent them home to think again'. The Scottish press had a field day, but what short memories they have. No mention of the taking of the goalposts at Wembley in the past or other times when the Tartan Army had a field day at the expense of the English. In fact, Piccadilly Circus was not a good place when Scotland were in town. The normal procedure was for authorities to board up the statue of Eros, as it was feared the Jocks would snap its base and try and take it back with them to the Highlands.

If Euro '96 and Euro 2000 proved one thing it was that the home fans had had enough and started to fight back, to the surprise of the Jocks. This was quickly pounced on by the press and as usual England were made out to be the villains, something the 'sweaties' were quick to back up. As for the match in Glasgow, the locals were shocked that an English firm had come up and taken the piss on their own manor. This was new to them and the message was out: 'enough is enough'. England were warned that any repeat of the trouble and it would damage their World Cup bid – a decision seen by many as effectively a done deal. FIFA and UEFA officials were already showing their dislike for the English.

The fact that two Leeds fans were stabbed and killed by Turkish Gala fans only fuelled the fire among the fans and when Turkey qualified for Euro 2000 calls went out among the English fans for an England united in Europe, seen by many as a way of revenge. Gala went on to the final and won on penalties. Trouble after the game was assured as the Turkish fans started on Arsenal fans – something which Arsenal lads did not take lightly. They retaliated, running the Turks all over Copenhagen. The stage was set for Euro 2000 and calls to bar the English fans went out.

Strict checks were going to be enforced on travel and 'known hooligans' were to be picked out and denied travel. No mention of the Turks who had caused so much trouble in the club scene and even killed two people. This was overlooked and once again England were seen as the danger. Again cries went out from officials for fans to remain calm and that trouble could damage England's World Cup bid. The eyes and ears of the press were on the English fans and such a hype was built up about them that the other countries' fans were forgotten. As usual, the press was to blame for a lot of trouble – they whipped up the fans in the press; anything to sell papers.

England's first game was against Portugal in Holland, and they lost 3-2 after blowing a lead. The press waited with bated breath for the fighting to start, but nothing happened. The odd scrap, but nothing on the scale the press were predicting. To say they were let down would be an understatement. They even said the reason was because the England fans were all stoned on the hashish that it is legal to buy in Holland and they were all calmed down by its effects. This may be so and many may have taken the odd smoke, but to say all were smoking it … any excuse as far as they were concerned!

They waited again for the next England game against Germany, a country with a large hooligan following and loads of right-wing activists. Surely their prayers would be answered there? Still no mention of the Turkish fans who had stabbed an English fan in Charleroi and early on at the Italy v Turkey game littered the pitch with missiles, bottles, seats and so on. No action was taken and again UEFA sat back and waited for the English to start the trouble with a 'told you so' attitude.

No mention of Turk fans attacking English fans after they had beaten Belgium 2-0. Local Turk youths attacked a bar that had been a gathering point for English fans – the English fans bit their tongues after threats of being thrown out of Euro 2000 hit home. This never stopped the Turks, who should never have been allowed to compete at all. The trouble was contained by Belgian riot police.

The local mayor blamed English fans, as they had started it off with previous flare-ups with Turkish fans during which English fans were killed. He even went back to the Heysel disaster, claiming that it was England's fault and making no mention of Juventus fans or the fact that UEFA held tickets that weren't for sale to the public but were on the black market – how did this happen? Only someone inside the UEFA headquarters could access these. Excuses were made and as usual UEFA wiped its hands of it and carried on with its warning – one more riot by England fans and they would be thrown out of the competition. To say UEFA is anti-English would be an understatement.

Of course, the press rumour mill went into overdrive with headlines of thousands of arrests. Later, a thousand fans were rounded up and deported (just for being English, many will say). Many had never been involved in football violence before or, if they had, their offences had been so minor they had never come to police attention. Many fans believed a hidden agenda was on the cards and they were right.

The World Cup bid was taken away from England and given to Germany (even though their fans had killed a French copper in the previous World Cup – but no mention of that!). There was also no mention of German fans fighting the English ones in the Charles II square in Charleroi. It was just reported that the English side were causing the trouble, when, in fact, it was a lot of slagging off, singing and a few plastic chairs being thrown. The response from the local police was way over the top and many would say it was set up to show the world England did not deserve the World Cup.

In fact, the locals had it all wrong – the Dutch seemed to have hit the nail on the head with how to deal with fans. They served the fans light beer, tried to keep them apart and it worked. The press were quick to state that it was the hashish that stopped the trouble, thereby labelling every English fan as a drug taker. No mention of the light-beer-only approach, something that the Belgians did not cater for.

Having a large crowd sit around all day in the hot sun drinking stronger beer than English beer had its effects. It was the spark they wanted and the England fans played right into it. Put it together with the local Turks and you have a recipe for trouble. Why did the Belgian Police allow the Turks near the square and allow full-strength beer to be sold on the day?

To put a game like England v Germany at such a small ground, when it UEFA, who steered thousands of fans into a town that never had the facilities to cope with the crowds, let alone hold a football match. Throw in the frustration, the heat and full-strength beer and it did not take long to kick off. Many England fans inside cafés – just fans with wives, girlfriends etc. – claimed the Belgian Police would kick open the café door and pump a pepper spray or gas inside. As many ran out choking, the line of police would whack them about with truncheons. Loads were grabbed, whacked with a truncheon, handcuffed and stuck in a tiny cell, then deported. Many were just in the wrong place at the wrong time.

Many claimed the police were frustrated as so many were arrested but no action was happening and they went looking for it. You would think with so many arrested it must have been a bloodbath – wrong! A few minor scrapes and a few plastic chairs being thrown. No need for water cannons and tear gas. If there was ever a prize for local Old Bill showing off to the world stage then the Belgians would get an Oscar. Totally over the top. Serving light beer would have stopped a lot of it, plus moving the game to a bigger ground. As UEFA had sold all their tickets this was not on the cards. After all, who wanted England to have the World Cup? No one except the English.

As it turns out, Germany have won the right to host it (again). A country that has many Turks living there and who are mostly not liked by the locals – let's face it, who does like them? There are many right-wing extreme groups there and I can see it being a success, no trouble at all (like fuck). They won't have to worry about English fans. Most of their trouble will be internal. The travelling English fans will not be the problem, though they are if you listen to UEFA officials. Gerd Aigner, chief executive, was quoted as saying Euro 2000 is a celebration of football, not an excuse for a small minority of English fans to cause havoc again. No mention of the Turks' behaviour, or the Germans', only the English.

While I agree there are some of England's fans that go way over the top, what about the normal fan who is confronted by an opposing fan, defends himself and is helped by other fans. Is he a thug or just protecting himself? Lord Bassam, a Home Office minister, admitted nearly all the fans deported were not known to the UK authorities. That proves one thing – that the Old Bill were grabbing anyone who was English and throwing them out of the country. Being English was a crime in itself when attending Euro 2000, according to UEFA officials – the same officials who sold black-market tickets knowing they would go to the fans they did not want.

The press did not help either – some buying weapons abroad, even guns, and handing them into police saying, 'Look what we could buy.' Anything for a story when, in fact, they were bought in England and they were nabbed at customs. I don't know what happened to them – talk of charges being laid was the last I heard. If they did, in fact, buy them in the UK, they should be made to reveal their sources. If they are so worried about football hooligans they would, but they won't, and I bet the people they got them off are in no way connected with football at all. Still, as I said, anything for a story.

The Turks had some rioting in Brussels but Aigner made it

quite clear that overnight trouble involving the Turkish fans in Brussels was in a different league to the English violence. 'They tried for a party, which turned into confrontation, but it was not an incident that could be characterised by unruliness in masses,' he said. Fuck me, a party went wrong. I note no English fans stabbed anybody, they were only on the receiving end of knives – used by whom? The Turks. If that was a party gone wrong, what will they be like when they are upset? Bring out the guns? What of their behaviour in the stadium? Was that a party gone wrong? Why weren't they threatened with expulsion from the competition?

There is a very united anti-English body within UEFA ranks. If UEFA were so concerned about English fans, why did they not limit the tickets allowed to the England games and use their own recommendations for weak beer only? Perhaps they would have lost money from ticket sales and other licence arrangements with other authorities.

You can't blame the bar owners. If someone is looking for trouble then it does not matter what they drink. The mob mentality, led by a few shit-stirrers, will kick things off all the time, no matter what country you are from. Take the Turks again. Having thrown everything bar the kitchen sink on to the pitch against Italy, they got a $4,000 fine. They did not stop there, according to the press. About two thousand went looking for English fans, wrecking a few bars on the way until finally being dispersed by riot police in the early hours of the morning. No mention of deportation for them, or threats of expulsion. Even after the UEFA Cup games, when English lads were stabbed and killed, what happened? Nothing. Had that been English fans, we would have been banned from Europe as in the past.

Time will tell. The next World Cup will leave egg on the face of UEFA and many a Turk will wish they had stayed in

Istanbul. It won't be the English fans to blame. Germany have many right-wing groups that make firms like the ICF and Headhunters look amateur by comparison. They will be on home soil. If FIFA treat German fans the way UEFA has treated English fans, then the press will have a field day.

I conclude by saying that most of the blame for the hooligan problem in Charleroi should be placed at UEFA's door. The fat cats of UEFA guided thousands of English fans into a small, hot, crowded area, where the only entertainment was to drink cold beer all day, just to wait for the match to begin. During the course of the day some baiting by other fans helped tempers to flare and their frustration was let out in the chair-throwing scene we have all seen on TV. Don't blame the fans – let's have a look at the organisers and the police again.

## CHAPTER ELEVEN
# SCOTLAND (THE SWEATIES)

Without a doubt, the Jocks are the biggest hypocrites around. They all mouth off. For example, at Wembley that time when they took the goalpost, or mobbed up in Trafalgar Square when they scared some tourists. When the England fans started to get it together and repaid some of the raids carried out by their Jock cousins and took it to them in Glasgow, there was an outcry. How dare they? The image of Glasgow as a 'hard city' was gone, and the English lads were quickly branded hooligans by the local media and anyone else north of the border. Fears for the Tartan Army travelling to Wembley for game two of the Euro 2000 qualifier were soon the talk of the town. They asked for and got police protection, and the usual large mob that had always turned up in force in London's West End was way down in numbers. Even the estimated many thousands of Jocks on the dole looking for work in London did not front up.

Things had changed. The English lads had had enough and decided to meet the so-called Tartan Army after taking it to the Jocks in their own untouchable (or so they thought) town. The same people who had been walking around London taking liberties were now on the soap box crying foul. They did not expect the English fans to fight back and when they did, on their own ground, they were shocked. The 'chip on the shoulder' syndrome came out and they cried foul.

At recent club games between Celtic and West Ham played at Celtic's home ground, which were a sell-out according to the officials of the Celtic club, only one hundred tickets were made available to West Ham fans. They made sure their own fans were looked after – fair enough, too. What they did not tell you is that only 35,000 tickets had been sold, including those for the travelling fans, and the supposed gate of 60,000 was well short of the sell-out. The reason was that they did not want a large group of English hooligans travelling to Scotland, so they banished all English fans and branded them as thugs. My, what short memories they have. Ask them about the trouble they have with their main rivals, Rangers, and they tell you that is different. Fuck me, a smack in the mouth from the opposition is a smack in the mouth – simple. Or do you have to be a 'Sweatie' to fight a 'Sweatie' at football? Then it is OK! Funny lot! A mate of mine sums them up this way (I reckon he was being too kind, but each to his own). He says:

> Scottish football fans must be an anomaly in the modern game, coming as they do from a nation with a fearsome reputation for grittiness, bravery and hard drinking. With a history of major sectarian-led hooliganism and general unruliness, their fans have in recent years developed a worldwide reputation for being good-natured party kings (along with their Celtic cousins from over the Irish Sea) of Europe.

*Whilst there is a certain truth in the Tartan Army myth it is only part of the story and there is a far deeper and wider spectrum of personalities that are associated with the game north of the border. From the unbridled bigotry and sectarianism of the Old Firm's more extreme followers to the more organised and in some ways chilling violence perpetrated by firms such as the Aberdeen Soccer Casuals, Hibernian Capital City Firm and Motherwell's Saturday Service to the ordinary 'barmy' army scarfer singing his heart out after ten pints of McEwans and not afraid of a row should one come his way.*

*Although you can't generalise about the Scottish fan any more than you could his English counterpart, there is definitely an added notch of passion with these folk that, aside from a few exceptions in the main hotbeds and big city areas down south, seems to be missing from the average English fan.*

The Jocks are quick to point out any victory over the English. They will often go back as far as Bannockburn in 1314 when they beat the English Army but forget to mention Culloden in 1746 when the English totally fucked them.

They will even tell you they beat us at Wembley 1-0 but fail to mention the 2-0 loss only the Saturday before. In 1967 they beat the English World Cup-winning side of 1966 and the Jock papers claimed them as world champs and said England should hand over the World Cup to them. They said England only won it because it was on home soil. I dunno about you lot but, when Celtic won the Euro Cup beating the Lisbon Lions, I was cheering for them, as they were British. Now being older – and, I trust, wiser – I hope they lose every game they play. They are quick to have a go at a certain ex-

Tottenham and England star about his drinking and bashing his wife but, when two or three of the Scottish team, including the captain, were barred from playing for their country because they wrecked a hotel one night, they were not so quick to mention it.

It used to be that Jock players came to England to learn the game. Then England started sending players up to Scotland to improve the League. Now it is 'spot-the-Jock'. Euro '96 was a classic example. The Jock press went into overtime when England played Scotland at Wembley and they tried putting Gazza off his game. Fuck me, he made them look silly with 'that goal'. It was 'Roy of the Rovers' stuff. The Jocks had no answer for him and it showed what a backward league they run up there.

If ever a Euro superleague is formed, or the two Glasgow so-called 'giants' were in the English Prem, I doubt they would last two seasons and they would not get into the top five. They only play four hard games a season up there and they are against each other. Out of the two, maybe Rangers would last. Then we would see what a travelling Jock mob would be like week in week out in with the big boys. Raising a large mob once a year is one thing, but to try and do it every week – they would fail.

The main reason teams like Celtic have so many fans all over the world is because of the religion thing. Who else would follow an Irish team in Scotland which is full of foreigners? If they were a Hindu team they would be lucky to get five hundred to a game. The Jocks talk a load of shite most times but these next few words sum them up well:

> *The rise of English nationalism has come on the back of rampant Celtic nationalism and separatism and, to sum it up, for some reason the Jocks are far more*

*passionate about England losing than they are about England winning. As the song goes [to the tune of 'Daydream Believer']:*

*'Cheer up Craigie Brown, oh what can it mean, to a sad Scottish bastard and a shite football team.'*

Just for the record, 'Flower of Scotland' was written by an Englishman.

Wake up, Jocks. You are only a Fifth World country whose main attraction is cold barren hills and a fictitious monster in a big pond. If the oil (which you don't own) was not there, you would be further down the tube. Stop giving the impression that you are all ex-Gorbals folk, it don't work any more. Stick to wearing your skirts and try and keep your jealousy of England under control.

## CHAPTER TWELVE
# MANCHESTER UNITED (GLORY-HUNTING C**TS)

Manchester United fans always leave me seething. This bunch of glory-hunting moaners are the equivalent of economic migrants, travelling from all corners of the country and the globe to bask in the reflected glory of the plc they follow. OK, let's be fair. There is such a thing as a real Mancunian United supporter. I have met loads in my time and had some good – and not so good – run-ins with them. I know a few outside of football and have had a few work for me. They are the genuine article. They are vastly outnumbered by the shower of pseudos that swamp the Salford every other week.

As Manchester City are the only official club in Manchester, with United not even in the main area of the city, there is a fair amount of feeling between the two, let alone the many other Premier League teams.

Like their southern cousins at Shite Hart Lane, these creatures are *never* wrong. Manchester United don't lose, they run out of time. All refs are against them and other fans persecute them and never give them credit (violin time)!

You would think that, given the amount of success they

have enjoyed and this intense feeling of 'us and them' that they espouse, they would be some of the most passionate, loud and feisty crowds around. Not a bit of it. Old Trafford is notoriously quiet when the Reds are getting beaten – even their manager has made comment on this. The only audible sound is deranged bleating about blind refs etc., mainly from the subs' bench. Well, that and the sound of footsteps as they leave the ground in their droves to get away from the rush and back to Kent or Cornwall.

The hooligan following at United have numbers – big numbers. Most are smack dealers having a day off to attend the football. On their day they are a formidable opponent for anyone but, like the rest of the fan base, they *never* lose. They have more excuses than a junkie avoiding rehab. They turn up at a different pub at a different time than arranged, claim a no-show by the other fans, say they bottled it and so therefore the day was theirs (oh please – come on, who doesn't want it with them?).

The Cockney Reds are a sad joke. Not content with the capital's thirteen clubs, they latch on to a northern giant whose real fans don't even want them. They are reviled around the land and good sympathy should not be wasted on the wankers. In short, I would not piss on these pretend fans who call themselves the Cockney Reds if they were on fire in front of me, and like the Yids they can fuck off and live their Walter Mitty existences somewhere a long way from me.

The Mancs are without doubt a rags-to-riches story. Having once had a great team of mostly home-grown talent (most of them were wiped out by the Munich air disaster), they have rebuilt in a way that most fans, including some Mancs, have contempt for. They now throw money at players and hope they win a few cups. The gamble has paid off.

A new breed of glory-hunting fans has started to appear in

the armchair set. They know fuck all about their club's history, but like them because they win things. Once upon a time a fair amount of football fans admired the way they rebuilt after Munich but now loathe them and their attitude towards the game.

They have conned the English FA into thinking they are too big for the UK and they think they have done the FA a favour by not joining a Euro superleague, while at the same time they pulled out of the oldest competition in the game, the FA Cup. Even their own fans were shocked by that. It seemed competing in a mickey mouse competition was more important. Their own fans mostly agree it was a shit comp. I dunno what they would have said if they had won it. They came back with their tails between their legs and said they did not take it seriously. Then why did they go?

They claim their players would have been too tired to challenge for the Prem. Fuck me, they have three squads of players who hardly play more than sixty minutes of football a week if they are lucky. Their main exercise on the pitch is chasing the ref around and moaning at him, or grabbing players by the throat (an offence for which a player should be red-carded).

Feelings towards the Mancs run deep and a lot came to light when their manager received a knighthood for winning the treble. I would point out that this has never actually been done by an English club – the treble consists of the League title, the FA Cup and the League Cup. They claim the League Cup is nothing and they only fielded a reserve side in the semi-finals of the FA Cup a few years back when they were running top of the League. In the final of the League Cup they were shouting they would be the first to win the treble; it was all over the papers worldwide. Shame Aston Villa ended that dream, but now they don't count.

Their fans have a habit of travelling to away games (mainly in London) then finding a pub, some miles from the ground, knowing full well there will be no opposing fans there. When they have finally caught Old Bill's attention after larging it up by giving elderly locals a hard time, they all get an escort to the ground. Then they have the cheek to claim a result. After most games the home fans are held up while Old Bill get the Mancs out early on to the coaches and trains and make their lives a bit easier, while all the time the Mancs are claiming a result.

As far as turning over another team's manor is concerned, they have a favourite trick they have been using for years. If they are two hundred- to three hundred-handed and find a small mob of about twenty to thirty they have a go and the small mob normally legs it – and I don't blame them. Then stories out of all proportion are put out by the Mancs about how they ran whichever firm it was.

Some years later they pulled off a unique treble, no argument. How many of you were going for the Germans that night? It took two players in the last two minutes to do something the so-called superstars could not.

On their return to Manchester a street parade was held. Now here we had the Prem winners, the Euro Cup winners and the FA Cup winners parading and it was estimated that about 650,000 turned out in a city of 3 million-plus people. Not a lot is it, when you consider that, when West Ham last won the FA cup, nearly a million turned out just for the FA Cup winners. Not bad for a city of 8 million and thirteen teams compared to 3 million plus and only two teams.

United's contempt for players clearly shows. They buy a goalkeeper, reportedly the best in the world, then spend a fortune on another keeper, then drop him and keep the first one going while they piss off the other one and keep searching for another one. Their reason for not keeping the Aussie – 'he can't kick back passes'. They called on an ex-Manc keeper from the Sixties to explain it to the fans. Fuck me, they never had the back-pass rule when he was playing, but he is now an expert. If he had been half as good as the Aussie he would not have been bad. He was one of the few keepers to have a keeper score against him from their own area. In the Sixties the Yids' keeper of the time did it and I think that England's most-capped keeper did it against a great former England keeper in a League match – but he won't mention that.

Anyway, enough of the team. Let's talk about their manager now. A man who, when he does not get his way with all concerned (the FA, the press, you name it), chucks a wobbly. He has said he would like to help the Scottish team but not manage them. He knows full well he couldn't buy players like he can in the domestic competition and therefore would fail, like Scotland usually do.

To say the Mancs are a hard firm would be a joke. Their main boys are good but the trouble is they have so many hangers-on from all over, even the so-called Cockney Reds, who mostly live nowhere near London. It gives them a false sense of security and makes them feel they are well hard, when, in fact, they are the laughing stock of the hooligan world. They will jump a scarfer at a station somewhere, about twenty-handed, give the poor sod a kicking and claim a result.

At Old Trafford it is different and they can mix in with some of the proper fans and again claim a result, when, in fact, they have been a spectator while the real lads had a go. I have been sent a few stories since my first book came out and quite a few are from lads who said they were there in 1967 when the Mancs took the title on our manor. We compared notes and I asked a few questions and they were pretty well right in what they had to say. I mentioned things that I did not mention in the book, things you could only know about if you had been there, and they knew. The only thing we did not agree on was the numbers the Mancs had. The fucking ground never held that many – to say they had 25,000 on the North Bank was a joke the whole fucking ground only held a bit over 42,000 and that was jam-packed.

The would-be Mancs were sorted and the few left agreed they had never seen anything so mental in their life. I had one lad contact me who was there. He says he came down with a load of mates in a furniture van and they parked up a fair bit from the ground and walked the rest. He said they were just past Upton Park station and they joined up with a load more Manc fans when they were pelted with bottles off the building site next to the station (it was about the time the Queens complex was built). They said they gave chase but never got them. He went on to say that inside the ground was the way I described it; he never forgot it and he has seen nothing like it before or since. He tells me that after the game it was like running the gauntlet getting back to the van, with fighting all the way to the station. When they did get back to the van they were met by about seven or eight lads who went about giving them a good slapping. There were only three of them at the time as the rest of his mates from the van got split up. They even put the windscreen in on the van and he was glad to get out in one piece. He told me that he has only been back to West Ham a few times since and every time he goes he thinks back on that match. He went on about some other Manc games, which I wasn't able to confirm so I won't mention them, but many thanks to the Manc fan anyway.

One old boy told me 1964 was bad and there was fighting all over the place in the FA Cup semi-final (which we won). I know there was trouble there because my old man and his brothers went up. You hear a lot when you are young.

The year 1967 seemed to be the start of the hooligan scene. Since then we have had many battles with the Mancs, some lost but many won. Here is a story about one lad's experiences at Old Trafford:

> They have often been called a souvenir company with a works team attached. They con the fans with a new replica strip every six months or so. In fact, I think it's nineteen in nine years. If they wear one and they lose more than one game wearing it, it is dropped as bad luck and the glory-hunting sheep believe this and buy another, thinking it will bring them luck. They have money to burn and use it to try and make sure they have the best players at all times to keep up their glory-hunting image. Just look at the current squad. They have more strikers than any other League club and if one doesn't find the back of the net in, say, sixty minutes, off he comes and they bring on fresh legs. This has been proven time and time again with the likes of the red-nosed Norwegian paper boy and the ex-Millwall/Yid c\*\*t who plays twenty minutes a week if he is lucky, and is happy as he knows the system they use will give him a good chance of personal glory and another medal on his chest.
>
> If Sir Taggart had his way he would want the game changed to match the Yank football – time-outs and change sides when the other team is on the attack. They said the Yank idea of bigger goals was the way to go. In short, they would fuck the game and the only

*interest they have is how much merchandise they can sell you. Many have complained about the tiny seating room at Old Trafford. No wonder they can squeeze so many in.*

The Manc support is massive, but their so-called hoolie firms are a joke. They do have some – in fact, a lot – of top lads, who can and will mix it with most, but the hangers-on, glory-hunting twats, fuck it up for them.

# CHAPTER THIRTEEN
# MILLWALL

Without a doubt West Ham's worst and most hated rivals are Millwall. The south-east London fans are one of the lowest forms of life that exist for West Ham fans. The two groups have hated each other from the days of the docks, well before the Second World War, and maybe even further back. A lot of it stems from the East India, West India, Surrey and Royal Docks, where gangs of dockers looked after their own crew and made sure any fiddle going was shared out evenly. This spilled over into rival football clubs and has been carried on through the years. Friday night 'offs' were always on between the two rival groups and anyone on the 'wrong side of the water' (the Thames) was to be eyed with suspicion and hatred. Those from the East End labelled those from Millwall as thieving gypsies, whereas the south London side viewed the East End boys as flash, smug gits and hated West Ham as much as West Ham hated them. Some have even called Millwall an East End team – that in itself is an insult to any Millwall fan and they are quick to deny it.

There is no doubt that the Old Kent Road area is a hard,

working-class area and a documentary on the Millwall fans, a *Panorama* documentary called *Treatment and the Halfway Line* shed some light on them. They seemed to crave the attention and set about trying to prove they were the lads to deal with. If Millwall were in Division One or the Premier along with other big clubs they would not have lasted. Maybe doing a few lower-league sides is about all they are good for, but when playing bigger teams they have come unstuck many times. They haven't the bottle to take it on week after week like teams such as Chelsea and West Ham or some of the bigger ones up north. The meetings I cover here are mostly between West Ham and Millwall and I cover one recent one where the Welsh lads Cardiff gave it to them even after all the gobbing off on how good they were. Some you will never have seen written about before, but they are true.

To kick off these incidents I will start with the death of a Millwall fan at New Cross station. No names mentioned, but he was a 'prat'. A group of Millwall lads had gathered at New Cross station hoping to pick off some West Ham lads on their way to the Valley, where they were playing Charlton in a League Cup game that night. Some three to four lads spotted a couple of West Ham scarfers on the train in a single compartment (a British Rail train, not a tube) and decided to lift their scarves and give them a slap for their trouble. What they did not expect was for the two lads to fight back – and they did, which shocked the Millwall a bit as the West Ham lads were outnumbered and Millwall had more lads on the platform who just stood there and never helped. Two of the Millwall lads had copped a good slap and jumped off, expecting back-up from their mates which never came. The third was trapped in the compartment and decided to jump out the other side door, but unluckily for him there was an oncoming train and he got hit full-on and was killed. The train never stopped and was pulled up at London Bridge. The Millwall lads pissed off while the West Ham stayed on the train and carried on their journey to the Valley.

Shockwaves went through the Millwall fan base and a fair few went on to Charlton that night to seek revenge, which saw them get a fair kicking at the hands of West Ham. To be fair to Millwall, they never had the numbers, but then again neither did the scarfers on the train.

Police reckoned the death was by misadventure and this certainly upset the Millwall following, who swore revenge. There were stories of whip-rounds in pubs and clubs – not for the family of the killed fan or wreaths, but so someone could do some West Ham lads. It was even rumoured that a couple of Millwall lads went over to West Ham High Street with a sawn-off shotgun to do some West Ham, but this never panned out and most reckon it was just Millwall giving it the large one and trying to scare West Ham lads – it never worked. Many terrace songs came out about this incident and Millwall went off the deep end every time West Ham sang them.

After the Charlton game the police were thick on the ground and many rode the trains back to London Bridge, where it was expected there would be a huge turnout from Millwall. There wasn't – they had not shown – and Old Bill stayed with the fans on the tube back to Whitechapel and on to Mile End, where it was rumoured a mob would be waiting. It was all bullshit. No one was around and the feeling amongst the Irons fans was one of bitter disappointment.

The two teams met each other in October '78. Millwall had sworn revenge for the death and days before the game leaflets were put around everywhere down the Old Kent Road. They screamed revenge for the death of the Millwall lad killed in the train incident. Police thought they were printed in Forest Gate and that it was a West Ham ploy to stir trouble. The leaflets had a photo of the lad killed by the train and went on to say: 'We have not forgotten you West Ham, this is the day we have been waiting for for nearly two years. For two years we have built up hatred towards those West Ham bastards'; it added that this would be no ordinary ruck – 'everyone who is done, is done for [name of deceased]'. Hammers fans were warned that any big trouble with the Millwall fans could cost the club promotion and even shut the ground. However, it had the desired effect.

Police were out in force, with over five hundred officers in attendance from Deptford and West Ham police stations, along with horses and aerial surveillance from a circling helicopter. At the end of the day there were seventy arrests and nearly as many chucked out of Upton Park. No doubt the massive police presence stifled the two groups' most violent intentions, but the worst premeditated violence came from the Hammers fans.

About half an hour after the ground and streets had been cleared of West Ham fans, police allowed the Millwall fans out under escort to the tube station. As they neared the Queens market about five hundred West Ham fans lying in ambush attacked and tried to burst through the police cordon, but a massive mounted police presence soon gained control and held the West Ham fans at bay. Afterwards a police spokesman said, 'These fans were like wild animals and I'm afraid in situations like this you have to treat accordingly. It was touch and go at times, but for the main part trouble was averted and we got the Millwall fans away safely.' He then went on to say the police operation worked out and everything went according to plan.

There was no doubt that Millwall shit it away from home and they did not live up to their name. They thought they were invincible after the *Panorama* documentary but that was just a myth and West Ham proved it again. The leaflet trick did work, but not to Millwall's advantage. In the paper there was a photo of Millwall fans getting an escort under the safety of the police. In one way, it was a shame that West Ham was not always in a lower league like Millwall because, if the fans had met season in, season out, a collection of books could have been written about the two sides' confrontations.

A couple of weeks later West Ham were playing Brighton at their ground. Rumours going around said that Millwall fans would be with the Brighton lads to get some revenge for the kicking they got a few weeks before. West Ham fans were well up for this one and thousands travelled down to the seaside resort. On arrival there was trouble from the off with another large group of fans who were, in fact, West Ham lads who travelled down by coach and car. It was soon sorted and the main target was Millwall, if, in fact, they actually showed. If not, the feeling was it would be a piss-take at Brighton's expense.

It started on the Friday night when West Ham fans turned over a seafront café and tried to set a boat on fire. This was the warm-up. The only casualty on the Friday was a local lad who was stabbed in the arm and back and slashed across the neck – for being a mouthy prat, it was said. Police made 96 arrests but the violence continued. Police confiscated knives, lengths of pipe, crowbars. Saturday was still to come and West Ham were anticipating the arrival of Millwall – however, it was a no-show by them and a big let-down. The Millwall fans later denied they had been going down. Many others will tell you they bottled it, simple as that. Another Millwall myth exposed.

After the Brighton flare-up the West Ham Secretary

disowned the West Ham fans after the havoc wreaked by them. He was alarmed by what happened and said, 'They are not West Ham fans, we don't want them.'

In '83/'84 West Ham were playing Millwall in the Southern Junior Cup final. It was a two-leg affair with the Den leg being midweek. West Ham had a firm of about one hundred and fifty that met up at Mile End and travelled on to Whitechapel. A West Ham ICF lad tells tells his side of the story:

> To catch the train out to New Cross or New Cross Gate, it was decided to go straight into the Amersham Arms pub and kick it off there. No one was around and we knew Millwall would be waiting but we set off again and headed towards Cold Blow Lane. It's a cold shithole and the walk to the ground is an eerie one.
>
> We caught a few locals on the way and they got a bit of a slap for their trouble, but so far no main mob, just a few strays. We cut across some waste ground near the ground and found a good-sized mob near a railway arch and most legged it, except one lad who pulled an axe and started waving it around. We stood our ground and chucked a few things at him, then we all ran at him and he dropped the axe and legged it. He was all front and we called his bluff.
>
> We got to the back of the Millwall fans' end and loads jumped the turnstiles to have a go at us – they turned around and went straight back in, as they were shocked to see how many we had. We had picked nearly as many as started out, and we was well up for it. The Old Bill moved in, and stood where the so-called 'halfway line mob' used to be. Not much kicked off during the game but after that we heard they would

*be waiting at Surrey Docks and we had our train filled with West Ham lads.*

*We stripped the train of every weapon we could find, seats and all. We decided to defend ourselves on the train carriage if such a big mob was waiting. The train pulled in and nothing. It waited for a while, then moved off. We later found out they had only a small firm, as most had bottled it and gave it a miss. Which just goes to show that reputations are not all they are made out to be. West Ham fronted on their manor and they bottled. The return leg was even worse with fuck all of their lads showing, but Millwall won't tell you about that.*

### THE BANK STABBING

A West Ham lad was stabbed with a sharpened knitting needle at the Bank and word had soon spread – we wanted the Millwall mob who'd done it but they had already left on their away train up north from King's Cross.

*The only way we would get them was after the game, when they returned. We had a mob of about three hundred to four hundred and we was on the prowl looking for them. This one Millwall lad we caught, a straggler running late for the train, was given a right kicking by a dozen or so Under-Fives. Old Bill moved in and grabbed the West Ham lot and when they found out it was a Millwall fan and he was one of the cowards at the Bank station stabbing they let them go and nicked the Millwall lad, even though he was lying on the deck well and truly fucked.*

*By the time the train got in we had about five hundred well-game lads and the Millwall lot got off chanting 'MILLWALL'. We gave the 'UNITED' chant back and steamed at them. The Old Bill never did a thing and they shit. They legged it across tracks, anywhere they could, as long as it was away from us. We caught loads and we went mental. There were Millwall fans crouching down screaming and crying. Fuck 'em, we gave them more. Some jumped the tracks and tried hiding in the freight/post carriage and hid out. We knew where they were and decide to get them after we had cleaned a few more up. We done them well and the post carriage was moving off now so we missed a couple but we never let matters drop there. Loads of us drove over to their manor and were well tooled up, but it was like a ghost town.*

*The following Saturday some West Ham chucked petrol bombs at Millwall lads at London Bridge station. West Ham chased them all over but Millwall were better at running than fighting and we never caught many. On the same day some Millwall lads were ambushed by a load of Under-Fives in their car on their way to Stoke. The lads and the car were wrecked and this was just a little payback for the West Ham lad who was stabbed. By the way, he was nearly fifty and stabbed several times, the weak c\*\*ts. Typical Millwall: all mouth and no show.*

A Millwall lad who was there that day tells his side:

*We knew what had happened and was sorta expecting West Ham to be waiting, but as the train pulled in they just surged on the platform. We put a 'MILLWALL' chant up but it was soon drowned out by the West Ham lads. I have never seen such a mad lot*

*Above*: Football fans in the days when the crowd was on its feet. My dad used to send me down to the safety of the front of the crowd.

*Below*: Glorious victory! Billy Bonds holds the FA Cup aloft for West Ham, following our victory over Arsenal in 1980.

Angry fans on the terraces and on the pitch.

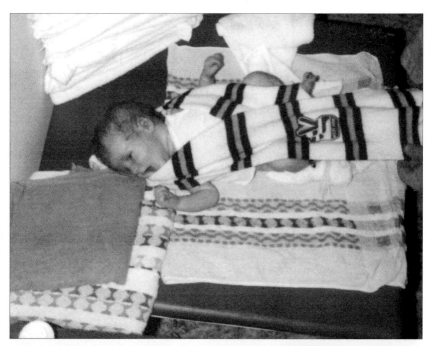

*Above*: My son, Chris, brainwashed from an early age. The scarf was bought at the 1975 Cup Final.

*Below*: With my daughter and son today. Although they have never seen West Ham live, they are Claret and Blue right through.

*Above*: The infamous Boleyn pub … enough said.

*Below*: West Ham main face Cass Pennant with Bob, a Canadian Hammer who travels over a few times a year to see his beloved team.

*Inset*: Cass by the famous statue of the 1966 victory.

*Above*: January 1992. Hammers fans protesting at Upton Park.

*Below*: A couple of Leeds Hammers with a local fan, celebrating the FA Cup win.
Cigars all round!

*Above*: Flying the flag for the Hammers in Europe.

*Below*: On the train to Celtic, members of the Internet Cyber Firm.

*Above*: The overwhelming West Ham support at Celtic Park.

*Below*: West Ham fans celebrate 'that goal' by Di Canio that knocked Manchester United out of the FA Cup.

*Above*: Terry Brown's MDF turrets.

*Below*: Internet Cyber Firm was one buyer of a brick in the new stand at West Ham.

*as them that day. Millwall got off and tried to run away to the furthest end of the platform and across the tracks. We jumped the tracks and got on to another platform and hid in a freight carriage. It was dark in there and we thought we were well out of it and we would just sit there till it quietened down. Some more lads came in and we asked who are you and they said Millwall. Thank fuck, we half expected a kicking. We sat in silence, then the train moved off. We ended up about sixty miles outta London before we could get off, but we were all glad we never got a kicking. It was after one in the morning before I got home. Fuck West Ham, I have never seen a mad mob like that till this day, and from what I heard off my mates the Old Bill turned a blind eye, the c\*\*ts.*

It seemed the Old Bill stayed well clear of the two lots of fans, and do you blame them? The Sunday press reported how the police had failed to protect the Millwall fans from the West Ham thugs and they were forced to flee on to the railway lines to escape the violence. Complaints from Millwall fans about how the police acted were noted by the Sunday papers. It just shows you how good they are. When they get a hiding from a bigger and better firm they run and call for police help, no mention of the lad who was stabbed with the knitting needle, when there was only three West Ham ambushed by a larger mob of the south London scum. Millwall like to think they can give it but they fucking can't take it and in my eyes West Ham have proven it many times. Millwall are a bit like Leeds – good for turning over small towns like Bournemouth in a lower league and feeling safe at home with the local Old Bill to back them up. But, away to a big team, they are fucking useless. Both teams have something in common – they are all mouth. The only difference is the accent, but both areas are much the same – Fifth World holes.

### 1988 AND PANORAMA

In 1988 a documentary about the London underground was shown by *Panorama*. It showed a bit of fighting between L*t*n and QPR fans, but it also followed West Ham fans on their visit to the Den. The camera crew, tucked away in an unmarked van, filmed loads of fighting as a large group of West Ham turned over the Millwall lot on the Old Kent Road. Listening to the commentary team it seems they were surprised that there was no Old Bill escort and the ICF was left to wander and have a go at any south London gypos at will. One of their stops was the Canterbury Arms, where a mob of Millwall were drinking. The ICF steamed the pub and it was all caught on film. To say the pub was smashed would be an understatement. One lad, a West Ham fan, said he was outside and it was going mental when a fucking big TV came through the window. This kicked things off even more and even the camera crew said, 'That's what you call West Ham taking the piss on Millwall's turf.'

Millwall claim they had it off toe to toe with the ICF shortly after they stopped filming, on a waste ground near the Den. That itself is a joke – the whole fucking area is a waste ground – but, in fact, most of their top boys were on their way to the Mile End tube to attack the ICF.

About two hundred-odd Millwall made the journey, only to find the platforms empty, so they went outside to the Horn of Plenty pub, a known ICF drinking hole, steamed into an empty pub and went about turning it over. Their fun had, they went back to Mile End station and ran on to the platforms chanting, only to find a large ICF mob waiting to catch the train to Whitechapel and on to the Den. This was the second lot of ICF who missed the first mob. To say Millwall were shocked would be an understatement. They got run at by the ICF; a few Millwall stood but were trampled. The main lot had it on their toes and away from the ICF lads.

The Old Bill piled in after complaints from the Horn of Plenty's landlord. When Old Bill showed, loads of Millwall stood behind the Old Bill giving it the large one again, saying they had overturned ICF's manor, when, in fact, they had trashed an empty pub. The Old Bill escorted the now gobby Millwall fans back to the Den and the ICF lads were made to wait. Word soon went out that Millwall were on the ICF's turf and Mile End station was beginning to fill. Old Bill had to let some of them go or there would have been overspilling on to the tracks.

Back at New Cross and the Old Kent Road, West Ham were having a field day. Having smashed up the Canterbury Arms and loads of Millwall fans, they went looking for more. When a large mob of fans came towards them, they ran at them, as did the other mob, only to find it was more West Ham from Mile End. Word soon went out more were on the way and this mob made its way to the Den. Millwall claimed they had a result, but they were caught out and the video evidence was on national TV. In fact, I have the tape and I piss myself when I watch it.

After the game Millwall tried it on again behind the safety of Old Bill, giving all the usual chants and trying to look well hard. It was proven that telling people they were hard on TV and wrecking towns like L*t*n is one thing but, when a game mob wanted to have a go, they were shite.

In fairness, they have some top lads but as with many clubs the mouthy hangers-on spoil it for them. Many of them live on the reputation they have worked on from the *Panorama* documentary. They thought they were untouchable.

One West Ham fan was killed in the West End one night. A normal fan, scarves, the lot. He was confronted by a small mob of Millwall, an argument broke out and the West Ham lad legged it down an alley. The Millwall lads chased him and stabbed him to death. They were nicked, taken to court and convicted. It shows you how brave they are.

Even though the two teams do not meet that often, loads of other firms claim a result against them. The 1999/2000 season is a classic example. The match between Cardiff and Millwall was the talk of the football world with planned meets arranged on the Internet, mobile phones etc.

Cardiff, by all accounts, have a fair firm at home and, living in Wales, having a fight with a rival mob other than the Swansea seems to break the monotony. My mate says he went to Wales once and it was shut, so a bit of fun at the football seems to be the remedy to brighten up their otherwise dull existence.

It seems Millwall did take two hundred to three hundred up there. After months of telling everyone they were going to turn Cardiff over with a mob of about eight hundred, only three hundred maximum fronted. The Old Bill were out in force and kept driving Cardiff back from them. Cardiff kept lobbing bottles, coins and anything they could get their hands on but there was no way Old Bill was letting Cardiff at them and they never seemed interested, just giving it all the gob from the safety of the ever-increasing Old Bill presence.

Just before the final whistle, at the end of a 1-1 draw, Old Bill started to let the Millwall mob out. The home fans could not believe it. Cardiff lads steamed into them and they ran back into the ground. Cardiff kept lobbing things at them and loads of bricks went over. The Millwall lot then charged the family stand and started getting under the main stand to get away. Cardiff again steamed in and Millwall got done bad and started to run. Soon Old Bill were on the plot and gained some control and they kept them apart for the rest of the day.

This was in reply to the time when Cardiff took down a fair-sized mob to the Den and took the piss all day in the Autowindscreen Shield. Millwall were well pissed off and swore revenge, something that backfired on them.

Millwall seem to think they are untouchable at home but have been proven wrong many times. While the area looks frightening enough, the fans are nowhere near the same and are only good at turning over little towns and clubs.

In the early Seventies, many a London derby, in particular the Yids and Rent Boys, seemed to start rumours that Millwall had teamed up with them. I have heard this many times, especially when those two have run again – they put the blame on the Millwall lot that was supposed to be there, something Millwall never own up to.

Going over to south London and the Den can be very dodgy on your own, but take a decent firm over and things are completely different. I have seen worse at Orient, but then again what can you expect from a team that lives in the shadow of West Ham and wishes they had the lads they have.

Many stories have done the rounds about Millwall. In fact, even the Scottish team Hibernian have claimed a result against them, which I note is never mentioned by Millwall. The Jocks took down nearly three hundred game lads to Millwall, some by train and coach, others by car, some even by plane. They planned to meet up in the West End and go to the Den as one large mob. On arrival at New Cross station they was no Millwall welcoming party – no one, in fact.

The Hibs lads walked down the Old Kent Road, before

turning their attentions to a Millwall pub. They wrecked the place and the Millwall lads inside – in fact, they took the piss. Some Hibs lads were lifted by Old Bill but most got into the ground, where they chanted and had a general piss-take of the Millwall fans. Chants of 'WE THOUGHT YOU WERE HARD' rang out but still nothing from the home fans. The match was a draw, and expecting some trouble after the game, the Hibs fans left together but there was no one there and they walked away untouched and disappointed. A few weeks later Millwall claimed they never thought the Hibs were coming down and weren't bothered by them. Typical Millwall – they bottle it then make excuses.

There is another story about the London Bridge station meet with West Ham lads. The West Ham lads had only a handful and were not expecting Millwall to be there. When confronted by a group of Millwall fans it was on, with the Millwall fans legging it one way and West Ham legging it another way. A petrol bomb was thrown at a wall, but nowhere near fans and some brickwork got a bit burned. The West Ham lads met up with a larger mob of ICF and went looking for the Millwall lads, hoping to find some more. They were never found. Some of the Millwall stories that came out of this incident were unreal – there were tales of a massive mob carrying axes, knives etc. It seems to me that is Millwall justifying their cowardice again. One fan says this about Millwall:

> I have been south of the river a few times and the Old Bill were always in control, but I have total respect for them since the first time I saw them at Upton Park in 1978.
>
> For weeks leading up to the game the papers were full of it. Some 22,000 ended up at the game, and

*every single one there seemed to be up for it. There weren't many dads with kids, mainly game lads.*

*The South Bank was filling up with West Ham very early. 'No one likes us we don't care' drifted down Castle Street. I was expecting 6'6" dockers, such were the stories I have heard of them, and the noise they were making did not make me feel any better towards them.*

*They made their way into the south-west corner of the South Bank and it seemed World War Three had broken out as a massive mob charged into them from all over, no quarter given or any taken. We were giving it our best and they were well outnumbered.*

*This lot wasn't running. I had never seen anyone stand their ground at our place before. They had about three hundred, maybe four hundred, but it was with sheer weight of numbers that we pushed them back.*

*More Millwall turned up and a three-way battle was on – Millwall, us and Old Bill. It was going off all over the South Bank. The west side attacked from the flanks as more and more Millwall came in. There were battles on the pitch, pure anarchy.*

*Pop Robson kept his head in a sea of pure hatred and scored all the goals in a 3-0 win.*

*At the end of the day they copped more hits than us but for the first time I had seen a mob not freaked out by the thought of mixing it with with our lot (mind you, it's probably bred into them down the Old Kent Road as we have it bred into us).*

### SONGS FOR MILLWALL

Some of the songs about the infamous train incident that came out at the time – a few different versions:

The first was:
>'West Ham boys, we got brains
>We put Millwall under trains.'

Then these few, to the tune of 'Whip Crack Away':
>'The New Cross train is coming on down the track
>(Whoo-hoo)
>And a Millwall fan is laying on his back
>(Whoo-hoo)
>He nicked a scarf
>And got cut in half
>Oh hip hip hooray, hip hip hooray, hip hip hooray.'

Another one along the same lines (pardon the pun):
>'The New Cross train come rumbling down the track
>(toot toot)
>And a Millwall fan's got train lines down his back
>(toot toot)
>He nicked a scarf
>And got cut in half
>Oh whip crack away, whip crack away, whip
>crack away.'

And this one:
>'They say the Millwall are famous and hard
>But the most famous one is now chopped in half
>Some say he jumped
>Some say he fell
>But the Millwall lad is now living in two separate
>hells.'

# CHAPTER FOURTEEN

# NEWCASTLE AND OTHER OFFS

Without a doubt the north-east boys are one of the most passionate firms around. Their rivals Sunderland (the Mackems), some thirty-odd miles away, hate the Geordie boys as much as West Ham hate Millwall, or Arsenal hate Spurs. They are a loyal, one-eyed bunch of lads, who have had a rough time in the Prem.

It took an old-age manager to stop them going down a division. The departure of their clog-wearing manager was a godsend to them after they thought they had cracked it with 'the clog on the Tyne will do fine'. Fuck me, were they wrong. They were glad to see the back of him, especially after it became known that their hero, home-grown England striker and captain was dropped by him and the two were not hitting it off. Bring in one old man, add a bit of ticker and bingo – your season starts turning around.

It is the events of the past meetings I want to write about, although I haven't a great deal on them. The Toon lads seem to keep a bit sturm on their activities, but one I will cover is the infamous firebombing with the ICF lads at St James' Park.

A West Ham lad gave me the story of what he saw that day:

*That game we went up to we came late and already missed the main crew. We were eighty-handed and thought we would be all right. We knew from past meetings with the Geordies it would be fun but we knew they did not shy away easily and on their manor they would be well up for it. The train got in and we all jumped off, only to find a big mob of them waiting for us. We were outnumbered badly and had nowhere to go so, fuck it, we went at them. The trouble was they went back at us and soon gave us a kicking, we were fucked. We gave them a fair run but they kicked the shit out of us in the end.*

*We found out the main mob had turned this lot over and they wanted revenge and they got it! After a while we got ourselves together and headed off to the ground. We linked up with the main mob and then we had a tasty firm. This firm was massive and had already blitzed the city centre. Shops were done in and their lads copped a right hiding.*

*When we were queuing up outside, one of the fuckers launched what we thought at the time was a petrol bomb. It kicked off again and the Old Bill were struggling to contain us next to the turnstiles. Midway through the game the c\*\*ts threw another petrol bomb into our section of the crowd and it went off, lighting a couple of people up. They weren't hurt too bad, but everyone went fucking mental.*

*We all went downstairs at half-time, as most did, and the two sections were only divided by some poxy fencing. The bogs were next to the fence and if you went for a piss you faced being hit by stones and bottles or golf balls. The West Ham lads were going mad. They were lobbing back as much as was coming over. This pissed off the Geordie lads, as they weren't expecting it.*

*After the game they were well away. Only a few stood and they got done badly. Old Bill soon sorted things out and we were walked back to the station. The Geordies had fucked off by now, which was just as well. We wanted them bad.*

Another incident of interest was the kidnapping of a Geordie fan. He was put on a chartered ICF minibus and taken back to London as punishment and left there with no money to get back. There was also some graffiti that appeared at about the same time at St James, Park that said 'Cockneys burn better with Shell'. I dunno if it is still there.

The Toons at home were a hard mob but not untouchable. They are one of the few firms who stand by their mates and will back them up. I have had quite a few run-ins with them at home and away. Some we won, some we lost. I know what they are like. The Mackems are much the same but I have not had any trouble with them, nothing major anyway. I respect both sets of fans as being loyal to their teams, unlike some.

One lad told me a story about a trip to Ipswich (the end of the road):

*Last time I was there was for a night match on a Bank Holiday Monday towards the end of the season. A small firm from Plaistow had gone up there for the day and they ended up in a snooker hall in the town and it kicked off with a gang of black lads. This little firm copped a bit of a slapping and were outnumbered badly. They vowed to come back after the game and* square things away when the numbers were a bit more even.

There was about forty to fifty of them who left the game early. We had beaten them again and we made our way into town. On the other side of the road there was this black lad walking along and one of our lot sussed him as one of the mob that had a go before. We all steamed at him and he pulled out some nunchukas and started waving them around. One of our lads grabbed a road sign and stopped the c**t from swinging them around and he copped a kicking. Then, closer to the snooker hall, we came across another couple of them and they wanted it, despite being well outnumbered. It got a bit heavy from then on in. We were at the snooker club now and mobbed up outside, but there was only one single door, a side entry into the place, and you could only get in one at a time.

We knew it would kick off but could not work out the best way to get numbers in there before it all got started. This one lad with us decided to rush the fucking thing and see what happened. We all got in and, as we opened the second door down the end of a small passage, the whole fucking snooker club was lined up against the far wall, all tooled up with sticks and snooker balls waiting for us to open the doors.

As we got in the bastards hit us with the lot. The lads at the front were copping it bad and tried to turn back but the lads at the back wanted in and were missing out on a good ruck. The fucking noise as we were trying to get in the place, it was mayhem. One of our mates dropped to the floor and we had to pick him up and drag him outside.

Not one of them wanted to come out – they were

*staying put, as they knew we would be waiting. Then some of our lot arrived from around the corner with two crates of empty milk bottles.*

*We waited five minutes and then re-entered the place, chucking the milk bottles at them. It was good toe to toe for a while for about two to three minutes (which doesn't seem a lot, but feels like it's ages), before someone yelled that Old Bill were arriving.*

*We fucked off quickly, back to the station. On the way home we found ourselves on the express train straight to Liverpool Street, where we knew Old Bill would be waiting if the locals up there had complained. As the train slowed near Bethnal Green someone pulled the emergency cord and we all legged it off the train.*

*Funny, you don't associate places like Ipswich with football violence, but there was some naughty people around that place.*

I had some stuff sent to me about the FA Cup semi-final at Villa Park between West Ham and Nottingham Forest. One person claimed the Forest lads hassled the Holte End and gave West Ham a right hiding. I was not there but remember seeing the game on the box and it looked to me like the West Ham lads were all over the place and were far the noisier of the two sets of fans. Even the TV commentator mentioned it during the game – I think it was Neil Warnock, who worked for the BBC, and he kept saying, 'Listen to them, listen to the West Ham fans' after nearly seventy minutes of 'Billy Bonds' Claret and Blue Army'.

One Forest lad I have been in touch with told me it was 50-50 on the Holte End with only a fence dividing the two sets of fans. A West Ham lad at the game said the same. He said the Forest fans were all on the Whitton End and outside there was a massive ruck between the two sets of fans, with both agreeing that Forest had been done real bad at the park outside and near the coaches. The Forest lad wrote:

> *They were fucking mental, they had just been beat 4-0 and had a dodgy sending off in their eyes, but their fucking fans went mad. Many of us hid our colours that day after the game. No one would have stood that day and the few silly fuckers who did were soon given a seein- to. We all stopped singing and taking the piss until we were well out of it on the coach. A few on our coach got a bit of a smack and they said they had never seen fans like it.*

A West Ham lad at the game said:

> *It was like a battlefield. West Ham just went mental and wearing red and white that day was not a good idea, as many found out.*

Which gives you an example of fans on both sides telling it like it was. I had some doubts when I first got this story, but a little checking and I found it to be kosher. Many thanks to both lads and to the one who tried to large it up saying Forest had a result – behave, mate, I doubt you were there and the story has been handed down to you (no disrespect to Forest lads).

Here is a story from a Bristol City fan:

> *I'm a Bristol City fan. I was never involved in any trouble, apart from being chased around Cardiff in the '73/'74 season when City was playing there. About*

one hundred of us off the special, chased by about five Cardiff fans (mind, they were bigger and older than us). But in those days I always got a thrill out of end taking and the chanting etc.

I was hooked on this, while visiting Cardiff during the '69/'70 season and my father took me to see Cardiff and Birmingham. Cardiff were riding high in the Second Division. Toshack was playing for them and there was a crowd of 21,000, I think. I stood in Cardiff's end (Grange End) and watched some running battles over on the side terrace (the Bob Bank). I think the two terraces were connected.

Never dared go to West Ham when Bristol City played there. Went to Millwall twice, that was enough for me. No trouble there but a place with a certain atmosphere.

I remember West Ham coming to Bristol City in '76/'77 (the game you didn't make it to). About two hundred West Ham in City's end (East End) made themselves known when West Ham's team came out. City's fans backed off, police moved in quick and took them around the pitch to open the end (Park End) where the rest of West Ham were.

I also went to the Watney Cup game at Bristol Rovers v West Ham '73/'74. About fifty West Ham fans outside the gates before they opened. When they opened they went in the Rovers end (Tote End), chasing Rovers fans out as they came in.

Rovers finally mobbed up and there were lots of rucks on the terraces. West Ham stayed in there all the game, although outnumbered. A police horse stayed in the middle of the Tote End all through the game.

# CHAPTER FIFTEEN

# THE CASTILLA GAME

The 1980/81 season saw West Ham qualify for the European Cup Winners Cup by beating Arsenal in the final of the FA Cup in 1980. European football was back for the West Ham fans and the first leg turned out to be an away trip to Castilla in Spain. Thousands of fans made the trip and in general were well behaved, until an event turned the crowd of West Ham fans sour – the death of a West Ham fan. This was not mentioned by the press of the day, who preferred instead to concentrate on the trouble caused by the travelling fans.

I will start with what the media reported, then continue with an eye-witness view from a fan who was there. He tells his story a bit differently, as you will read. The return leg was to be played behind closed doors at Upton Park, with UEFA saying any attempt to let the fans in would result in West Ham being thrown out of the competition.

West Ham played the home leg with only the playing staff and a few stewards in an empty ground. Already down 3-1 from the first leg, many thought West Ham's European Cup matches would soon be over. Playing a home leg in a ground with no support would surely see them lose, many said. In fact, West Ham turned a 3-1 deficit around to win the two-legged round 6-4 on aggregate, winning the home leg 5-1 with Pike, Goddard and Cross all scoring, and Cross bagging a hat trick. Parties went on all around the ground, while many fans waited outside and listened to the radio or packed the pubs and waited for the final whistle. It is said you could hear the players shouting to each other outside in Green Street and the whole night was eerie to say the least.

What caused this situation was the first-leg game in Spain. UEFA said the game must be played at least 187 miles from Upton Park, but after an appeal from the West Ham board it was decided to play a locked-out game at the Hammers' ground. The then supporters' club chairman insisted that even if the game was played a thousand miles from Upton Park it wouldn't matter as travelling Spanish fans would meet real trouble if they came to the game. He said there was a feeling of subdued ferocity against the Spanish at our game on the Saturday. Everyone blamed them for starting the trouble. He said that, wherever the game was played, no doubt our lads would get there, and stated: 'It's a personal opinion, but if the Spanish fans turn up it will be murder. I think they should be banned from coming over.'

The West Ham board were concerned that the UEFA ban, coupled with a £7,000 fine, had been imposed without the club being able to state its case. The West Ham Secretary of the time said, according to figures he had, only a handful of people were involved and there were only two arrests. They wanted to put this evidence to UEFA's disciplinary department, and perhaps an appeal would have given us a chance. But as usual UEFA's comment was: 'We have taken this action because of the provocative behaviour of West Ham fans. We regret that West Ham were not personally able to put their case but that was not technically possible because of the time involved. We are now determined to stamp down on the problems of the English supporters.' Sound familiar? Roll the clock forward to Euro 2000 and you would think I was talking about that. No mention of the West Ham fan killed, just like the two Leeds fans killed by the Gala fans. Only blame the English – simple. The sooner we get the anti-English members off UEFA's board, the sooner we might see some decisions going with England and against other countries. Until then, what hope is there for the English fan?

To compound matters the West Ham captain of the time made a statement in the papers under the headline 'YOU SCUM'. The report went on to say that drunken West Ham fans had dragged soccer's reputation deeper into the sewer. In Madrid, it went on to say, some of the fans who had followed West Ham to the European Cup Winners Cup tie behaved like scum. They urinated on Spanish fans from a tier of the magnificent Bernabeu stadium during the 3-1 defeat, pelted the pitch with empty beer bottles and ran around the terraces punching and insulting local supporters. They battled with riot police, who charged them with batons, and in doing so these pigs kicked the West Ham skipper in the teeth (which pigs? Do they mean the Spanish Old Bill? Can't see West Ham fans doing their own captain, can you?). The captain then had written to every supporter travelling to the game asking them to behave themselves. He was choked, he said, and asked what could you do about such animals. He said that they wanted support at West Ham – but not from fans like this. His saddened manager said, 'We took every precaution possible, then this happens.'

So even the West Ham captain and manager got their two bobs' worth in and blamed the West Ham fans. Still no mention of the West Ham lad killed by the Spanish. He didn't count, it seems. To say that fans battled with riot police who baton-charged them is wrong and is well out of order. That would only upset the fans more because they had a policy of looking after their own. Other fans may have legged it and I think this was the riot police's main aim, but they, like so many before them, underestimated West Ham fans, who stood. This shocked them and if they hadn't had riot batons they would have legged it themselves. As usual, English fans were the cause again. *Still* no mention of the fan killed. I mean, he was only English. I would bet if an olive eater had been killed it would have been different. A mini Heysel, with the Spanish fans absolved of the blame.

This is the story from a fan who was out there at the game. You can judge for yourself:

### CASTILLA – A FAN'S STORY

*There is one game that has not been covered, perhaps because there were only 2,500 West Ham fans there, but since it resulted in the death of a fan it is strange no one has written about it in depth. I am referring to the visit of West Ham to the Bernabeu stadium in Madrid where we were to play Castilla in a European Cup Winners Cup tie back in 1980.*

*During that time you wouldn't really consider travelling to a European tie under your own steam and therefore we arrived at Upton Park at 7am on a chilly September morning to begin the journey to Madrid. There were many top boys on the coaches as we headed for Gatwick. The flight was a noisy one, the first time many of us had travelled to a competitive European game, and everyone seemed in fine voice. On arrival in Madrid we dumped our bags at the hotel and went in search of a bar. There were plenty around the city centre and we heard of a few skirmishes but* nothing major. The stadium was quite a way from where we were staying and we needed to take coaches to get there.

As we entered the stadium we found ourselves high up on the terracing and, in a stadium that held 120,000, the 30,000 crowd looked quite sparse. However, to put things into perspective, Castilla were, in fact, Real Madrid's reserve side, so a 30,000 crowd to watch a reserve game wasn't bad. All was fairly quiet as the game began, until far off to our right we could see the local force laying into some West Ham who were in the wrong section. Immediately the atmosphere seemed to change and we were aware of an increasing police presence in our own section. The trigger for trouble to follow was a West Ham goal. As David Cross dived to head us into the lead, the Guardia Civil went into action, hitting anything and everything with their batons. I turned and saw a bloke who was there with his wife and young daughter. As one of the officers went past he hit the bloke's wife – obviously the bloke went apeshit and as he started to hit back, helped by many around him, reinforcements were called for and the entire situation started to get out of control. I saw one lad I knew as Joey get hit and fall to the floor under a baton. One of the lads threw himself over Joey's back to take the blows, which just seemed to bounce off him.

Once they had tired of raining blows they moved on to find more easier pickings as the lad picked himself up and checked Joey was all right. The next hour or so was a case of watching your back as the hostile atmosphere increased. The effect was felt on the pitch as West Ham conceded three goals to lose the leg 3-1.

*Once outside the stadium it was a question of trying to find a coach to take you back. The Spaniards themselves started throwing bottles and kicking off the odd one or two who had been separated from the main mob. I was with four other lads as we boarded the coach and it was surrounded by diegos banging on the windows. The coach driver looked terrified as one West Ham lad told him to open the doors. As he did three Spaniards boarded and the doors were shut behind them. Whether brave or stupid, I don't know, but they were battered to fuck before being bundled out of the coach. We sped off towards the city centre and went back to the hotel, cleaned up a bit and then headed back to the nearest bar. We met with some more West Ham already in there and one of the lads was talking about seeing a West Ham fan being hit by a Spanish coach. As more lads joined us in the bar the story was that this bloke had died after being rammed up against a wall.*

*After four hours of drinking and swapping stories, about twenty of us left the bar about 2am. Now I don't know what it is with the diegos, but as we were walking back to the hotel a couple of them started giving us a bit of verbals. After the night we had been through, it did not seem like a wise move. A couple of the lads ran over and kicked the shit out of them and, thinking they had enough, came back. It seemed as though these lads were game enough, though – they picked themselves up off the street and from what we could gather asked if we wanted some more! This happened twice more, before the diegos had decided enough was enough, although the sound of sirens heading towards us made us realise that it was time to move on!*

The following morning we got hold of a copy of the *Sun* before heading off to Madrid airport. The back page contained a one-word headline: 'SCUM'. It went on to say we had battled the Spanish Guardia Civil and confirmed the fact a West Ham lad (name withheld out of respect) had been killed. We could hardly believe what we were reading. For most of the time we were simply defending ourselves and the West Ham captain was quoted as calling us scum. The return journey was in complete contrast to the outward leg, with a deafening silence as we all reflected on the events of the previous night.

The following Saturday saw us in a home game against Watford. During the warm-up our captain approached the west side, to a chorus of 'Bonzo, Bonzo, we're not scum', to which he replied with a two-fingered salute. He was booed throughout the game despite a 3-2 win, and I don't think his relationship with that section of the fans was ever the same again.

The resulting investigation by UEFA into the trouble in Madrid found West Ham to be the guilty party. Despite the fact that a West Ham fan had been killed, we were the ones taking the blame. Sound familiar? Initially we were ordered to play the second leg two hundred miles from Upton Park but, given the fact that, thousands were prepared to travel, the decision was taken to play the game behind closed doors. We were warned that if there was any trouble or if the fans tried to get in to see the game, West Ham would be thrown out of the competition. Apart from an attack on the Castilla team coach at the Beckton flyover, there were no problems.

*The night the match was played we decided to get as near to the ground as we could. We went into the Boleyn pub and listened on the radio in there, where the landlord had set up some speakers in the bar. It was a strange occasion, with a total attendance of 263 you could hear the players calling to one another and the commentary was almost impossible to make out. West Ham scored three times in the second half to take a 4-3 aggregate before conceding a late goal to take the tie into extra time. Two more goals from David Cross gave him a hat trick and West Ham the match 6-4 on aggregate.*

*The following week saw a march to Downing Street being organised with a petition being handed in for an inquiry into the death of the fan. The march was from Mile End station and attended by a crowd of 2,000, although we were not allowed near Downing Street – after all, we were just football hooligans. The truth about what happened was never uncovered and Thatcher's government did not really give a shit. To them it was just a case of a hooligan getting his just desserts.*

*The scene today is very much different to the way we used to know it. Prearranged meets are now the order of the day, rather than taking a firm on to your opponents' terrace. The game itself has changed beyond all recognition and, while I take my own lads to sit down in the relative comfort of Upton Park, I can't help but feel sorry that they will never know what it is like to stand on the terracing, swaying with the crowd, sometimes your feet not touching the floor. When you talk to some people about the way it used to be and some of the things I have seen, you can see the look of horror on their faces, but I would not have had it any other way. Those years following West Ham were the best and I will never forget being part of it.*

So there you have it. A regular fan's story about what happened in Spain and the English fans to blame again, even though an English fan was killed. Roll forward to Euro 2000, or the 2000 UEFA Cup. Two Leeds fans killed and UEFA again blame the English. To say UEFA is anti-English would be an understatement. It could not be blamed on their organisational skills or the black-market tickets sold which were only supposed to be held by UEFA officials, or even as far back as Heysel when they were told the ground was not fit to hold the final, let alone segregate the fans. Did they listen? Did they bollocks. But when the deaths of the diego fans happened, who got the blame and who was nicked for it? Not the diegos, they were blameless. All I can say was that they were lucky it was Liverpool and not, say, West Ham, Millwall or even Chelsea. Things would have been worse for sure, as the liberties taken by the diego fans would have been well stopped and not allowed. Liverpool fans in general are a well-behaved lot but were cornered and came out fighting and the diegos did the thing they do best – *run* – which resulted in the stampede which caused all the deaths. Well done, UEFA.

So: Castilla, Euro 2000, UEFA 2000, Heysel – wherever there is trouble, let's blame the English.

# CHAPTER SIXTEEN
# THE OLD BILL

A subject on which everyone has a different opinion. Unless you have had first-hand experience with them (and I don't mean a parking or speeding ticket), you really wouldn't understand. You may have some sympathy for them. I don't. I know they are a necessary evil but sometimes they go way over the top and who better to vent their anger on than the football fan/hooligan.

You have heard from one lad about his banning order and how Old Bill got up in court and told a different story from what he said had happened. He admitted to being involved in fighting but that was not enough for the police. They painted a completely different picture and no doubt would have been happy to see him go down for half a stretch (six months).

Without doubt they are faced with a hard job at the football and often you see five or six Old Bill grappling one lad. Because the lad does not want to be taken he struggles and the Old Bill cannot punch him or lay the boot in while in the public eye, especially today with so many CCTV cameras around. They save it for later, out of the way of prying eyes and in the comfort of their factory (police station), only to say in court that the accused resisted arrest and that's how he copped the many bruises he has. Some of the coppers involved have the same stories down to a word, and the fucking magistrates believe them because the evidence against the lad is overwhelming. I mean, he is a football hooligan, isn't he? Not some lad who was attacked by another group and tried to defend himself.

The police have a way of bending the truth. They are not quick to tell the truth in many cases and, as long as the result stands for them, they don't care. Many a magistrate hands out light sentences to people who the Old Bill think should get jail and when they don't the 'why do we bother' attitude comes into it.

At football matches the police use horses and dogs and in Europe they are worse. I think we are lucky the Old Bill are not armed (although a lot carry firearms you never see, like their foreign counterparts). I dread to think how many shootings there would have been at football by now.

Some police forces are worse than others, of course. The South Yorkshire Constabulary is one which has come in for a lot of recently. I have had a couple of run-ins with this lot – nothing major, and mainly at Leeds. They copped a fair amount of flak over the Hillsborough incident because they left the main gates open to let the massive amount of fans who were outside in, which triggered the crush on that fateful day.

Everyone blamed each other, from the Old Bill and the Sheffield Council right through to Thatcher for putting the fans into 'pens' and bringing in the ID card scheme. Senior police escaped prosecution as they were not to blame for giving the order. The judge, a Mr Justice Hooper, ordered a stay on proceedings against senior police. One senior officer's counsel said it put unfair pressure on the man's family. Fuck me, what about the families of the 96-odd that were killed? Someone gave the order to open the gates, causing the flood of fans and their deaths. But who? If there was ever a classic case of closing ranks, the Hillsborough disaster is it. The day that changed football for ever.

A Fulham fan died at a match a few years back and the police were quick to blame the hooligan element when he fell, hit his head on the kerb and died.

Now the anti-hooligan bill is in, the police are rubbing their hands with glee. They have a free hand to stop and detain someone, or stop someone travelling if they suspect him to be a football hooligan (or a scapegoat for anything they want). The English fan has been painted as some super-hooligan by the press and the police and the Home Office listen to them.

Euro 2000 was a classic example of overzealous policing, with so many arrests of English fans and hardly any of the other fans. No wonder the lads over there got upset.

UEFA said it was England's fault, so that was that. It wasn't the fault of the Turks, who, in UEFA Cup matches only weeks before, had stabbed and killed two Leeds fans. They had stabbed an Arsenal lad in Copenhagen and regularly pulled knives, among other weapons, on England fans and provoked them. They were having a party, according to UEFA. Did the foreign Old Bill do anything? Did they fuck!

A classic case of this kind of attitude came after the Heysel disaster. I think there were eighteen Liverpool lads who were arrested and deported back to Brussels to stand trial while all along the Juventus fans had kicked it off. It was clearly seen on the TV. The fans were not kept apart and this caused the trouble. There were also grown Italian men, three- or four-handed, kicking the shit out of some twelve-year-old scarfer and, when the older Liverpool fans came to help, what did the diegos do? The usual run, which caused the stampede and the deaths.

Many of you would have seen the aftermath on the TV, during which a Juventus fan ran out and fired a pistol towards the Liverpool fans. A fucking pistol – why did he have that? Makes you wonder. Were there any Juventus fans arrested? Was there fuck. Only Liverpool lads, and our government stood by and let it happen. It makes me laugh. If you are a football fan then you are automatically branded a hooligan no matter what your job or even your age, but if you are a convicted terrorist from Northern Ireland then you get released from jail. It isn't going to get any better either, believe me.

# CHAPTER SEVENTEEN

# TOTTENHAM HOTSPUR (THE YIDS)

If there is any team that lives for glory and has tasted it slightly it is the Spurs. The great Spurs sides of the Sixties were graced by players like Gilzean, White, Greaves, Blanchflower and many more. They were the first English club to complete the domestic double, and the first English club to bring home a European trophy – the ECWC. Since then, nothing much has happened. An odd Cup win and the odd Cup loss.

The fans believe the glory days will return. They have waited so long that they have become deluded to the point that they still think they are one of the 'big five'. In fact, nothing could be further from the truth. To sum them up, they are a bunch of deluded wankers whose last calendar appears to have been purchased sometime in the early Sixties. The Yids have the same arrogant attitude towards their team as their cousins up at Manchester United, without any of the justification. Yid fans are never wrong about football and will never concede a point until it has whacked them across the head a couple of hundred times.

They have had some good players in the past – good, not brilliant. Most Yid fans believe in the return of the glory days. A prime case is Ginola, who was considered the greatest by them until their manager decided he wasn't wanted and the chairman finally opened the purse strings and brought Rebrov into the side. This excited the Yids and soon talk of glory days was on again, as thought they had only lapsed for a short period. They had something to get excited about, but only time will tell on this front. I can't see it.

Their star player (by their standards), Sol Campbell, would not a sign a new contract and it appears he held out till the end of the season for a Bosman transfer and collected the money himself. Why not? Best of luck to him. The new manager at the time went to Leeds, where he had a short stay before being enticed to the Yids. His first season saw them lift the Worthington Cup in a boring game against Leicester City and the fans were talking about Europe again. They were quick to point out that they were in the UEFA Cup and they reckoned it would be an easy task to bring the silverware home. How wrong they were.

I have been to many a Yid game, against my side and other London teams. I have been cut by them and of all the London mobs they are the only ones who have a go now and then, mainly at home though. I have seen them play Chelsea in a FA Cup final and the Yids had the day. Back in 1967 when the skinhead scene and football hooligans were becoming noticed I saw Chelsea walk right around their ground, White Hart Lane (or Three Point Lane as I call it; some call it Shite Hart Lane) and they were not touched, let alone fronted. In the ground it was a Mexican stand-off. I was disgusted with this.

There was another match where Chelsea were chased on the pitch and they still believe to this day that it was solely down to them when, in fact, a fair mob of West Ham lads were present and kicked things off.

I have been to Highbury and watched the so-called famous north London derby with Arsenal and I was shocked at the attitude of the Yid fans towards the Gunners fans, and the feeling seemed to be mutual. To say they hated each other would be an understatement. I could not believe they were the same lads who were fighting; we only wished they would put up a show like that with us. Out of the two, the Yids were slightly in front, but not by much. The Yiddos were a handy firm but they thought they were too good and came unstuck many a time. I have had first-hand experience with them, and after I left the country I was often told tales of their exploits.

As one West Ham lad told me:

> *I have got a few stories of our north London mates. Mostly the Yids, but a few Arsenal scum as well. You should understand I was never anything approaching a face at West Ham and I never considered myself a member of the ICF. My main aim was to support the team, although I went into opposition territory on all local derbies at their manor. I did my bit when called upon but was quite happy sometimes when nothing went off. Just as long as we did not get done or showed up. So lots of my stories are just what I remember. There were loads more lads more active than me and may have seen some of the incidents I tell you about, maybe a bit differently.*
>
> *You mention the Yids in '76, one of the few games we both attended, and I was always under the impression they had a pop at the North Bank (knowing full well most of the main lads were on the*

*South Bank). They weren't there long, and they got the shit kicked outta them by the Under-Fives, yet you say they put up a bit of a show and stayed all game. You obviously knew a lot more than me and I don't doubt you for a minute but it goes to show how differently you can view things from different areas of the ground (mind you, I wasn't thinking straight, as you will read later). So, although I am more than happy for you to use this in the new book, remember I was no great authority on what went on, it's just what I saw or was involved in.*

*July 2, 1976, Tottenham away at Shite Hart Lane and I was fourteen and decided to go with a mate from school who was a Yid (sacrilege I know, but we all make mistakes). Anyway, the plan was to grab a train south to Tottenham, go to the game and stay with relations in Edmonton. Being young and super-naive, we wore our teams' colours all the way up there. My mate was saying, 'When we get to Shite Hart Lane, hide your colours.'*

*At Tottenham we came across a mob of two to three hundred who were roaming around, turning over the local shops. (Oh shit, I thought. My mate was as happy as fuck: 'Told you to hide your colours, Spurs are well hard,' he said.) They looked the part as much as anyone could in '76, with the stupid high waistband flares which was the fashion of the time.*

*We got around to the ground and came across a mob of Yids trotting round looking for West Ham. Ten minutes later it had turned into a sprint in the other direction. They had found what they were looking for and the original mob we saw turned out to be West Ham wearing no colours.*

*My mate was gutted. 'Better hide your colours, mate,' I smugly told him. It was my first sight of the Yiddos (one which I would see repeated over the years), their backs getting smaller and smaller in the distance, but far from the last. I ran out of fingers and toes to count the amount of times they had it on their dancers.*

*Once inside, the first mob teamed up with about another two hundred and roamed the place the way you could at Shite Hart Lane, taking the piss on the Shelf, the Paxton and the Park Lane. Every time the Yids had it on their toes, they never stood once and loads got a good slapping.*

*After the game, which ended in a 1-1 draw, West Ham had a massive off and ran the Yids all over. Even my mate copped a right-hander on the walk back to Edmonton. 'What were you saying about the colours?' I pissed myself laughing, he was well pissed off.*

*My second encounter with the Yids was November 6, 1976. We had the Yids at home. The day began in the worst possible way. My granddad lost his fight with cancer that morning and the last thing I should have felt like was going to the football, but the family said I needed to get out and take my mind off things. So I went and it was the Yids so, fuck it, why not. I walked down Green Street and about a hundred Yids had gathered outside the Boleyn pub. One Yid ran out of Nathan's Pie and Mash shop with a piece of cutlery inserted in his neck.*

*There were big rumours of the Yids on the North Bank but we doubted that as the last time they tried that they got a real kicking on a night game that had a floodlight failure. In the darkness all you could hear was Yiddos getting turned over. But it was true enough*

*– we all ran around to get on the North Bank and see for ourselves. Sure enough, there was a mob of them on there singing away and fuck all West Ham. We all got in and surged towards the fuckers; they scattered and a few tried to stand but got a real good slapping for their trouble. There was plenty of rucks going off as the game went on but it seemed to calm down as far as we were concerned. The Yids had been sent packing without too much fuss (like I said earlier, a bit different to your version, Mick).*

*Then again, the loss of my granddad in the morning and the fact the Irons seemed hell-bent on another season of struggle put five past the Yids and I was not thinking straight. I had so much hatred in me after what had happened to my grandad and then the Yids tried to take the piss on our manor – I had had enough!*

*January 1, 1977, pissing down with rain, no trains, fucking big hangover. The local coach company ran coaches to Yid land and I got there late, it was 3.10 pm. I reckoned we were bound to take the Paxton again and as we queued up to get in 'Chim Chimerney' was being sung. It's ours, I thought. My mate reckoned they were singing, 'We hate those bastards in claret and blue'. The rest of us thought he was a c\*\*t. We got on the Paxton just in time to see dear old Trevor give us the lead. Celebrations were cut short as it was payback time for the Yids. Fuck me, that hurt and a Happy New Year to top it off. The silly fuckers managed to snatch defeat from the jaws of victory.*

*Old Bill got us out and I told myself I would not cheer for another goal on an away end again when so heavily outnumbered. Well, not for another four years anyway.*

*1978 Testimonials. I vaguely remember two, one at each ground. Only a few hundred turned up at Upton Park. It was Bonds' testimonial and on the way out after the game West Ham lads were out lining Green Street as the Yids ran the gauntlet. In the away game we turned them over in the Seven Sisters Road forty- to fifty-handed. They did not last long as we surged towards them; we dropped a few and the rest had it on their toes – mind you, they did put up a bit of a show.*

*In December 1978 our trip to L\*t\*n was off. We decided that five of us would take in the north London derby. We went into the Shelf as neutral observers, bit like the UN. We could have done with the blue helmets they wear.*

*The Yids got thrashed 5-0 and we were the ones smiling in the Shelf. It was pure hatred as the sea of red in the Park Lane celebrated. I have been to a few old firm games and they were tamer than this. The Yids were so up for it outside, the Gooners were slaughtered. The skies were full of bottles, bricks, anything that could be thrown and could do damage to a Gooner skull and any West Ham that happened to be nearby. My mate was not impressed with all the blood on his new shirt or the six stitches needed that night.*

*My mate from Glasgow was coming down for the match in December 1980. I met him at Euston at 4pm and we walked past about ten Yids. I thought they had sussed us but we were not wearing colours. Mind you, a Cockney Rejects badge helps you to get rumbled – the Yiddos shouted a few insults, then left us alone.*

Down at E13 outside the Queens the Yiddos were being picked off. Then a mob of about three hundred-odd Hymies turned up. They looked a tasty firm and plenty of glasses were being chucked. We were soon into them, just a chant of 'ICF' did a fair job. A few toe-to-toes, but soon we were chasing the fuckers around the market place.

Into the ground we went and into the west side. A resounding version of the national anthem went up. It sounded great and was followed by a 'sieg heil' (these were the days of the British movement at West Ham). A few Yiddos I know who were in the South Bank said it was some sight and it got them a bit concerned for their safety, but not for long. A mob of about a hundred ICF waltzed in there among them and kicked it off big time. The Yids were running everywhere.

My mate from Glasgow was amazed. We decided to follow the Yids back to Forest Gate station. Us on one side of Green Street, the Yiddos the other side. In the middle were Old Bill pushing the West Ham lads back and trying to protect the Yiddos. One of our lot went flying through a plate-glass window followed by a sniping Yiddo mob, scattering glass and saris everywhere. Little groups of West Ham shifted off down side streets to avoid Old Bill, but by the time we got to the junction of Green Street and Romford Road our numbers had halved.

The Yids suddenly got brave and charged at us. Amazingly, most of our lot were on their toes. We had a few one-to-ones, but the Yids finally got a result – not something easy to live down.

I wanted to apologise to my Jock mate and explained that the main faces were still down side streets, but now and again you have to accept a loss even by those scum. Still, we had done the Yids 1-0 and took the battle to them in the South Bank. My mate who was there reckons the only reason the Yids had a go when they did was because our numbers were well down and most Old Bill had pissed off inside the police station up that end of Green Street, knowing that if they were going to get done again they could pile in there.

April 1981, the Yids were playing Liverpool at Shite Hart Lane. What a day – such a laugh you missed out on, Micky. Our Inter-City train was on its way to Sheffield. We stopped at Leicester and about twenty of us got off to find an off-licence to get some drink for the rest of the journey. They had stopped selling drink on our trains for some reason. We came across a mob of Leicester who mouthed off, then legged it when we fronted them. We then found out our game at Sheffield Wednesday was postponed, so we took the next train back to London.

We decided to go to Shite Hart Lane and take in the game there. Finally back in London, we made our way over there and Old Bill were using a loud-hailer telling Liverpool fans to go on the right-hand side of the Park Lane. There were about three hundred to four hundred West Ham in the left side who had the same idea as us and Old Bill had sussed us out and put us in the other side of the Park Lane where they could keep an eye on us.

We were copping loads of abuse from the Yids in the Shelf. They were furious that we were there and taking the piss big time – 'You are surrounded,' they sang; 'We surrender,' came the reply and we were chanting 'PLO' at the Yids, getting on our knees and praying to Mecca.

The Scousers looked on in amazement at the four hundred-strong conga going on (it looked good on Match of the Day *that night, shame I did not have a VCR in those days). At half-time the Scousers came up to the fence and asked for our help outside. We obliged them and when we got out we got the golf-ball-bottle-throwing exhibition, nowhere near as impressive as what the Gooners got in '78.*

We had taken a massive liberty and the Yids were well pissed off. There was going to be a few more bad days for the Hymies before the end of the year.

Same month, we were away to Grimsby. I dunno if you have ever been to Cleethorpes before you left England, Mick – what a fucking depressing place. About three hundred plus were at St Pancras, along with five trai loads of Yids en route to the Cup semi-final at Hillsborough. We were well outnumbered but still strolled around like we owned the place.

That night back at St Pancras we were as happy as fuck, having won our last piece of silverware to date, the old Division Two. Word had got around that it had kicked off at Brixton (the riots) and Old Bill were thin on the ground at the station. A perfect chance for the Yids to have a go. They did not seem interested – perhaps it was our reputation. I could not see them hanging back if we was Arsenal.

We met the Yids in a two-legged Youth Cup final. First game at West Ham and the Yids were in the South Bank, not many but one is way too much. A few of us at half-time went via the bogs and up into their bit for some action – a few offs, nothing much.

166

Word was going round that a small group of game Yid lads were jumped a few miles from Upton Park, but we all know they can outrun our lads, so a bit of innovative thinking was called for. There was a taxi rank nearby, full of cabs. The ICF travelled the odd mile, leap-frogging the Yids, then met them again. By now they were totally fucked, having legged it for a while, and then ran straight into the West Ham lads they were running from.

The second leg, at their manor, West Ham were everywhere and hardly any Yids. We had a little set-to in the Shelf, but Old Bill soon calmed it down.

2nd September, 1981, back in the old First Division, some two hundred-odd boys from the Horn of Plenty pub headed off to White Hart station via Liverpool Street. As the train pulled in a mob of Yids were hanging around. A massive off followed. They seemed to be on top for a while, then Old Bill turned up and the Yids legged it, but not before breaking my mate's nose. He was swearing revenge and, to add insult to injury, he got nicked as well. A few of us hung around to see if he was going to be released. The original mob from the pub had gone so we decided to head off on to the Shelf, the destination talked about in Mile End. Our arrival had not gone unnoticed. Old Bill had put the main lot in the Paxton. We ended up on the Park Lane, only half a dozen of us, and we kept our heads down.

The game was a few minutes old when Dave 'Psycho' Cross scored. The Park Lane went mad, but we kept sturm as we were a bit outnumbered! It was funny listening to what these Yids wanted to do to their East End cousins, not knowing half a dozen of them were so near by.

The PLO flag was unfurled and the Yids went crazy. In the second half, amazingly, we scored again and then again. We were 3-0 up, a dream and we had to keep sturm.

Psycho scored a fourth, that was it, we could not hold it in any longer! We cheered like fuck and then waited for the incoming hiding like we got in 1977 – but nothing happened. We were shocked. After they spent nearly ninety minutes of screaming for our blood, and then a 4-0 hiding on the pitch and a perfect chance of revenge and there was not a punch. If there was the lottery that night we would have won it and been rich. Psycho scored all four and I had been deep in the enemy territory, heavily outnumbered and not so much as a slap.

Funnily enough, he did the same at Grimsby earlier in the year (have I mentioned what a shithole Cleethorpes is?), and I was outnumbered in the Grimsby end. Plenty of ICF in the side terraces and thousands of allies on the opposite end. Grimsby knew we were there but did not have a pop. Our reputation had gone before us and they kept waiting for a mob to come in with the numbers to turn them over.

In 1984 we were at home to the Yids. We were heading towards the Earl of Wakefield when a massive roar went up. Apparently the Yids had come in around the back streets but a mob of ICF found them and borrowed the contents of a builder's merchants and used them on the Yid fuckers. By the time we got there Old Bill were racing to the scene and a lot of dazed Yids were picking themselves up off the floor.

In the main I have a lot of contempt for them. A few I know are very handy in a row but in a mob they *were, or are, fuck all. Any offs, we were taking it to them. Although they certainly put on a show against the Arsenal in '78, it pisses me off when they adopt their 'big club' attitude. Although I have to admit I owe a lot to a small firm of Yids in Crete.*

*Not long after the Heysel incident, when being English abroad was not a good thing, there were six of us outside a bar. The place was full of crumpet, a few Man United, Leeds, Bolton etc. and about eight or nine Yids. The bar got attacked by forty-odd Greeks, apparently because one of them had been given a slap in a club that night. We were the third bar of English to be attacked that night. They were well tooled up and the doors of the bar slammed shut. The northerners disappeared, as did some of my mates, leaving the four of us and the Yids. 'Fuck it,' we said, and steamed into them. They weren't used to this and soon legged it, but that little mob of Spurs restored the Yids in my eyes.*

*Judging by the sites on the web, they are finally getting their act together. They even had some boys in the west side last year. There are a few other stories I could tell you but my eyes are killing me, Micky. Like I said, it's just my personal view based on what happened and what I was involved in. Others may not agree but there you go.*

So there you have another account of one person's meetings with the Yids. He admits to getting done now and then and there is nothing wrong with that. If only all other 'firms' were so truthful.

A few years ago the Yids were West Ham's first game and their main boys said they were going to teach the ICF a lesson. They did not show – in fact, about sixty to seventy of their so-called lads got turned back at Whitechapel for their own safety, and the few who did make it mixed in with the scarfers on the Centenary Stand (the old North Bank), as per usual, gave it all the gob. It was good to see West Ham's scorer in the 1-0 defeat run up to them and kiss his West Ham badge on his shirt. The same season Arsenal were to play the Yids at Shite Hart Lane, a north London derby. Feelings of hatred were running high as rival fans wound each other up over the Internet.

The Gooners arranged to meet in the Prince of Wales pub on Tottenham High Road. It is right next door to the Pleasure Rooms, a well-known Yid hang-out. The Arsenal fans did not give a fuck about their rival cousins and it just shows how much contempt they have for them, drinking in the pub next door.

About a hundred Gooner fans had gathered and no Old Bill were around. When the Yids found out that the Gooners were next door, some nine to ten vans were parked outside. The Gooner numbers had risen now to about one hundred and fifty and not one Yid fan tried to have a go at them. To say Arsenal were taking the piss was an understatement. Just before the game the Old Bill escorted the Gooners to the ground, a short walk, and the Yids were giving it all the mouth, knowing full well they were safely tucked up behind Old Bill. A few bottles were lobbed, but no serious damage. The Yids went on to win the game 2-1 and after the match the Old Bill kept the Gooners back for a short while, mainly because the Arsenal lads were well pissed off. OB wanted the Yids to get away first. The plan worked and only a few scarfers hung around after. A couple more bottles were thrown by the Yids but, again, no damage done.

One Arsenal lad tells it this way:

*The Yids did not want to know. We just took the piss*
*on their manor and they could not stop us. We never*
*had great numbers and they claim a result. If throwing*
*a few bottles is a result then they are in serious trouble*
*when it does kick off.*

### THE TOTTENHAM 'MYTHS'

#### 1. The Year Ends In One

Well, another great Tottenham myth has finally been put to
bed. All this 'year ends in one' nonsense which made Spurs
fans think they were some sort of blessed outfit is nothing
but confirmation that Tottenham can't do any more than
win an occasional cup every ten years or so. The only thing
that ended in one in the North London derby was the Spurs
scoreline, and they should count themselves lucky that
their bitter rivals didn't have a scoreline of double one! It
would not have been unreasonable for Arsenal to have
knocked up eleven goals against a very weak and uninspired
Tottenham team.

I wonder what sort of reaction George Graham would have
got if it was one of his teams that had put that performance
together? But the blinkered faithful would continue to
worship the great Hoddle and forget any mistakes he makes
because 'He's Tottenham through and through' Playing an
unfit Campbell was one of the biggest blunders they ever
made. Eventually they saw the light and sacked Hoddle.

#### 2. We Want Our Tottenham Back

Have you seen the state of those tossers from SOS (Save Our
Spurs) who campaigned so hard for the removal of Graham
and Sugar? And what does all this 'We want our Tottenham
back' actually mean? Which Tottenham is it? It's commonly
acknowledged that the Spurs they want is the one under

Ardiles who apparently played this 'Champagne Football' that you hear mentioned around north London. Well, let it be known that the Tottenham side playing this brand of football were notoriously hounded and abused by Spurs fans after one shameful display and defeat at the hands of Notts County. But don't be surprised by this, because in-fighting is part of the great Spurs tradition. This is a football club who decided they would not retain the services of its greatest patron because they didn't want to pay him a nominal fee for scouting, despite him offering his services to the club he adored. Bill Nicholson was the last great Spurs manager, but the club shamefully dumped him on the unemployment list because they couldn't see fit to retain the great man, even on a small wage. This, in fact, caused great friction with a number of Spurs players past and present and was one of the reasons for Steve Perryman walking away from the club.

The bitching between Sugar, Pleat and Graham was not unique in the history of this sad club. Pleatt has recently had the cheek to blast some of Graham's transfer dealings while they worked together before he was sacked by ENIC. Yet Pleatt is the man who bought one Italian player that turned out to be the biggest load of crap ever to pull on a Spurs shirt! And he cost them a few million in transfers, wages and final settlement. Turns out the player wasn't even good enough for our Second or Third Division clubs! Pleatt bought him on a recommendation.

ENIC have already shown their true colours, and I don't expect it to be too long before they eventually fall out with the current management and/or playing staff.

*3. Spurs are one of the top five*
This is another wonderful yarn, manufactured around north London. Not quite sure how this one evolved, other than

that Spurs fans truly believed that should break-away European leagues be formed then they should be included because they are 'one of the top five'. Well, they are not one of the top five supported clubs in this country, so it can't be on crowd figures. Furthermore, they have failed to even register a top six, let alone top five, placing in the Premiership since it started! In fact, those Spurs fans who harp on about 'We want our Tottenham back' will do well to remember that it wasn't that long ago that they were playing their football in the lower divisions. Failing to register a top six finish in the ten years that the Premiership has been running is a disgrace, and dismisses this myth.

*Summary*

The one single factor that keeps me endlessly amused is this self-importance that all Spurs fans heap upon themselves and their team. They are nothing but a mid-table outfit, unable to compete with the Manchester Uniteds and Arsenals of this world. (There you go, there's another reason why they are *not* a top five club.)

They have consistently failed to finish in the top three London clubs for the past three seasons, and this season will be no different.

The more bullshit these Tottenham types throw up, the more I laugh. Please, please, please keep it up, Tottenham fans, you make my world a happy place on a daily basis.

# CHAPTER EIGHTEEN
# **THE BOND SCHEME**

A West Ham fan tells about the failure of the 'Bond Scheme'
and what can be achieved when fans stick together.

> *The game I grew up with has changed beyond all
> recognition over the last fifteen years or so. The influx
> of money from Sky, the formation of the Premiership,
> the Taylor Report and all-seater stadia – all, in their
> own way, have driven something of a wedge between
> the grass-roots supporters, and the clubs they loved.
> The pricing structure of many Premiership clubs now
> means that many of those who stood on those terraces,
> on cold, wet, Saturday afternoons, now find the cost of
> going to games prohibitive. However, football clubs
> that take their fans for granted, in some cases treating
> them with contempt, are nothing new.*
>
> *Some ten years ago, as the plans for all-seater
> stadia were being drawn up, several clubs attempted to
> take advantage of the reduction in ground capacity, to
> extort money from their fans. A debenture scheme was
> introduced, whereby purchasing a 'bond' from the club*

would guarantee you the privilege of buying a season ticket. Let me say that again: purchasing a 'bond' from the club would guarantee you the privilege of buying a season ticket – not the actual ticket itself, merely the right to buy one!

There were three clubs pioneering this 'bond scheme'. They were the Scottish champions Glasgow Rangers, English Division One Champions Arsenal and my own club, West Ham! Yes, West Ham, those perennial underachievers, a club who had won nothing in the preceding ten years (nor, indeed, would in the following ten years), were attempting to take more money from their loyal support, on the premise that, once ground capacity was reduced, there may be difficulty in getting in to see the games. Although there was no fuss made in Scotland, and little it has to be said from Highbury, those of us who had spent a fortune following West Ham up and down the country, home and abroad, were not going to take it lying down.

The prices being charged for the bonds ranged from £500, of which there were only a few, to £1,000, which was the vast majority of bonds available. The protests that followed are still talked about today. A show of 'fan power', on a scale rarely seen before or since, began at the club.

My brother and I did our bit for the cause by bringing along banners to every single home game, each one different. The first was unfurled in the North Bank at Upton Park, and read 'Wanted: For the murder of West Ham United' and went on to name the Board of Directors at the club at that time.

This brought the campaign some media attention, as it was featured on the front page of football magazine

*4-4-2, and we were up and running. This continued with banners being unfurled in the 'Chicken Run' in full view of the Directors' box; probably the most famous one simply read 'Lying, Thieving, Cheats'.*

*The Hammers Independent Supporters Association (HISA) was formed, with some prominent names at the helm, with meetings held in the Denmark Arms, East Ham, to discuss plans of action. However, planning was always difficult, since feelings ran so high that the majority of protests were spontaneous acts by individuals.*

*Although there were demos after virtually every home game, one of the defining moments of the campaign came during a game when somebody jumped over from the 'Run', picked up a corner flag, marched into the centre circle, plunged it into the ground and sat down. This was the cue for hundreds of fans to flood on to the pitch, from all parts of the ground, and the game was halted. Standing right in front of the Directors' box some three hundred or so fans just sang at the top of their voices, 'We won't take this shit no more!'*

*This act moved the campaign on to another level, as the protests forced the club into making concessions to those wishing to buy bonds. Bondholders, it was decreed, would get the first opportunity to buy tickets for all West Ham games, would have their own association, which would liaise with the Board of Directors, and – wait for it – would have their own page in the match-day programme!*

*Despite the growing ferocity of the protests, the club seemed intransigent, and it was a single act on the final day of the season which brought the episode to* an end. As the crowds left Upton Park for the final time, a group of about fifty fans gathered on Green Street. The target was the club chairman, Len Cearns. As he approached the exit to the car park he saw the crowd gathered on the opposite side of the road and tried to speed away. However, one guy actually threw himself in front of the car outside the Boleyn pub, and as the brakes were slammed on the fans gathered proceeded to kick the shit out of the car. Although he pulled away, the car was caught again as he turned left into Barking Road, and chased until he was out of sight. Within two weeks the chairman had resigned his position.

So who actually won the battle? Actually, there were no winners, only losers. Although the sale of bonds was a disaster, the entire scheme was underwritten by the Royal Bank of Scotland so, regardless of how few West Ham sold, they were guaranteed not to lose money. However, what they did lose was something money can't buy. The bond, that blind loyalty shown by a great number of fans for generations, had been broken, and nothing would ever be quite the same again. Those who ran our club had shown nothing but contempt for those of us that turned up, week in, week out, regardless of the quality of the football on offer, by wanting us to put yet more of our hard-earned cash into our club, yet get nothing in return. In my opinion this was probably the bleakest period in the history of West Ham United, but what those of us who protested did achieve was to ensure that no other clubs would ever consider such a 'bond scheme' again.

## CHAPTER NINETEEN
# CHELSEA (THE RENT BOYS)

In late 1976 Chelsea were to play Arsenal in the League Cup (now the Worthington Cup), Fourth Round, at Highbury. A few of us heard that a fair mob of West Ham lads were going over for a night out. I agreed to meet up with some at Tottenham Court Road station. I thought about a hundred-odd would show. In the end there was no more than seven of us, but we decided to go anyway. Loads of Chelsea and Arsenal fans were on the tube but no real mob so to speak. We decided to go on the North Bank and see what transpired. The ground was nearly full that night and no sign of Chelsea lads as yet, with less than twenty minutes to kick-off. We thought, as per normal, a no-show by them. Arsenal were singing 'Chelsea, where are you?' – and to our surprise a Chelsea chant went up behind us. About eighty to a hundred lads were there but not for long; they were steamed on all sides by the Arsenal fans, who gave them a good kicking.

Chelsea fought back, but in vain, there were too many Gooners for them. Old Bill moved in and it just settled down. We thought it was the calm before the storm – surely there must be more of them on there? Having a go on the North Bank with so few was madness, but that's all we could see. Loads of blue and white on the Clock End, but here just a small mob of hardcore or silly c\*\*ts, having a go, totally outnumbered.

They copped a fair kicking. Some Chelsea lads moved away and a couple filed past us trying to look like they weren't there. One of their lads sussed us and asked if West Ham were here – my mate told him we had a massive crew and was waiting till the game was over and we were gonna team up with Arsenal and do Chelsea bad. He looked shocked; we never saw them again, or the Chelsea fans. It was all a piss-take. Arsenal had done them good and needed no help from us. After all, we were seven-handed and just enjoyed being spectators for once.

Arsenal won the game 2-0, and on the way home we heard tales from groups of Chelsea lads on how they'd run the Gooners. We could not believe it. Chelsea were claiming a result when they got the shit kicked out of them. Some lads at work had heard they ran the Arsenal, and it was a massive off. Nothing could be further from the truth: Chelsea got done, simple. What did they expect with only about a hundred-odd on the North Bank at Highbury? At our next West Ham game loads of lads heard West Ham were there as well – so the Chelsea rumour mill had gone into overdrive. At least they didn't claim to do West Ham as well – not on that occasion, anyway.

We had an Arsenal lad at work and he heard West Ham was teaming up with Chelsea. Nothing could be further from the truth. The only West Ham there I saw was the seven of us. The truth be known, we never threw a punch and Chelsea got done by the Arsenal all by themselves, no help needed.

I have to admire Chelsea for taking such a small mob on

the North Bank and letting them know they were there, even if it was short-lived. We found out later there was a lot more on the North Bank but they never helped their mates. That was bang out of order. Why go on there in the first place? To let your fellow fans down was bad, no excuse for it. That is an example of something you will not read in any Chelsea book, even though they claimed a result.

Around Christmas that year, Chelsea were at home to Fulham – George Best was playing and also Rodney Marsh. About four of us went along to see them on a freezing cold day. We stayed clear of the normal pubs we knew Chelsea used and kept our heads down, sorta. Outside we saw a few Fulham fans get a kicking – not real lads, more of your scarfers, but they were attacked all the same. We thought, fuck it, and went on the Shed End. We saw a few faces we knew and we figured it was a bad move once word had spread that West Ham were on the scene.

The lads who saw us were the proper Chelsea lads and at half-time had a talk to us, quizzing us why we were there – they wanted to know how many we were. We told them there were loads of us all over and if Chelsea kicked it off we would join up and it would be on. We would be Fulham for the day. This had the desired effect and we had no trouble at all. Getting done by a mob who were Fulham for the day did not appeal to them, and they knew they could not live it down, when, in fact, it was all bullshit and they swallowed it. We told them we were here for the game only, that was if nothing happened and they kept sturm about us.

As we all left after the game we saw a massive Chelsea mob running towards Broadway station looking for Fulham lads. There were none in or out of the ground, only a few older types with bobble hats and they were getting a bit of a touch up; we were disgusted. Fulham never really had a mob of lads then, and to turn over a few scarfers was bang outta order, but that's Chelsea for you.

The Chelsea lads have claimed many a result against other teams' firms, but will never own up to a defeat. I have gathered loads of stories from both sides and even had some accounts from fans who were there but support neither side. Chelsea will always be quick to tell you about how they turned over West Ham at Parsons Green station, when, in fact, there was lots of fighting, but claiming a result was way off.

First the Chelsea fan's account of this:

> *Fucking West Ham. We had already done the ICF when the train pulled in. The doors would not open so we lobbed what we could though the windows. The Hammer c\*\*ts were lying on the floor screaming, they did not want to know us, the cowards. There was blood and glass everywhere. Some West Ham tried to get off but we battered the fuck out of them. ICF shit – we showed them who are the Kings of London ...*

This from a West Ham lad:

> *If you call smashing a load of train windows while West Ham fans can't get off as having a result, then well done, Chelsea. At Parsons Green you attacked a trainload of kids and scarves, real brave.*

So who do you believe? It's a fact West Ham were attacked at Parsons Green station, but there are conflicting reports about what actually happened.

I got this from a Millwall fan, and for a Millwall fan to stick up for West Ham is something quite rare. I tend to go along with his version:

*A few of us decided to go over to Stamford Bridge as there was rumours going round of a big off with the Sunderland and ICF lads, along with Chelsea lads. ICF were all outside the Stamford Arms, when one of them blew a whistle. You knew then it was on. The ICF mob steamed into the Shed boys queuing to get into that end. Chelsea scattered and many were screaming out. The ICF then turned and went down the packed Fulham Road to meet the Sunderland fans. West Ham charged and Sunderland did not want to know – think they were confused by all the ICF shouts and whistles going off. The Old Bill rounds up everyone, including me, and takes them on to Fulham Broadway station and on to Wimbledon.*

*One trainload was gone and the next train came in – it was packed with scarfers. A mob of Chelsea threw everything they could through the windows. While many lay on the floor, they never opened the doors and we were stuck inside. My mates and I were well pissed off – if we were going to cop a kicking from Chelsea because of West Ham, we wanted to have a go back, but there was no way we could get off. A load of lads were on the deck crouching down to avoid the glass and other stuff flying around.*

*They still never opened the doors and a few lads tried getting out between the carriages but had the shit kicked out of them. At last the train moved out and many on the train wanted to get off and go back at the next stop but Old Bill was on the plot and the train was held up at Earls Court.*

*West Ham never got done that night – I would say if they did as I hate the bastards, but at the Bridge the main ICF lads took it to Chelsea on their manor and had a result. Not a big one but none the less a result. On the train it was mainly kids and shirts, no real lads. If that had been the train before things would have been different with the main ICF lads. Chelsea got a result by smashing up a train and scaring some kids – but doing West Ham? No way, Micky. I would like to have seen it happen, but I was on the train and that's what went down.*

So a Millwall fan and his mates tell a different tale. I know who I believe and it's the Millwall lads. Why would they lie? They hate West Ham with a passion. Just one of the many versions you hear.

In my experience with Chelsea there has been the odd time they done us – like at Upton Park station when the Old Bill closed the gates and trapped some West Ham lads on the platform who had got there early to catch Chelsea out – it backfired and they got a kicking. Fair enough, but the stories that went around about Chelsea turning over the whole of West Ham are not true. They gave some lads a bit of a kicking, but that's all. Funnily enough, West Ham will put their hands up to it.

Another example is the ICF documentary on the television in the mid-Eighties, *Hooligan*. It clearly shows West Ham and the ICF lads on Chelsea's manor, even though the game was at Upton Park. West Ham never had a big result that day and were outnumbered, but not many got a bad hiding, getting back to West Ham only to find the police had escorted the rest of the Chelsea lads right into the ground, where as per usual the 'all gob approach' by their lads came into play. The video never lies and Chelsea claimed a massive result – what a joke. Regardless of the 'camera never lies' scenario, ask any Chelsea lad and they will tell you different. Bending the truth has always been one of Chelsea's favourite weapons when it comes to supposedly having a result over the opposition.

The following is a story about a Friday night drink one lad and some Gooner mates had in the late Seventies:

*We lived out Hounslow way and used to meet up for a drink in the Honeycombe pub on a Friday and see who was going where for the match. We had been doing this for a long while, when one Friday night a group of about twenty lads came in, got a drink and seemed to settle down. As the night went on the 'Keep the Blue Flag Flying High' started, along with a few other Chelsea chants. One of my mates told them to shut it, when this one Chelsea bloke screams at him to get outside and they all bolt out of the door, taking glasses and what they could with them.*

*We grabbed some pool cues and balls and followed them out into the car park. There they all were, giving the large one, when this one geezer jumps forward and says, 'I'll have any of yer.' A mate of ours, a black bloke, just laid into him. I reckon three to four hits and he was fucked. The others just scarpered, leaving him there. We were about fifteen to sixteen strong and we never gave chase, just took the piss. This motor pulled up and out jumped this lad screaming 'Chelsea' and waving what looked to be a iron bar. We steamed him and got the bar off him and laid into his car with it. He copped a good kicking as well. I must admit he had front, but it did him no good.*

*We never saw the rest of them again and we went back into the pub. We were sort of expecting them to come back well tooled up. The first bloke who got a good slapping came in, and he was covered in blood and wanted a taxi. We all took the piss, and asked where his mates were. He just looked blank, and we never saw him again. We heard that Chelsea were well pissed off at getting turned over and were coming back but we never saw them again – all mouth and front that lot.*

I have been told that story by a few lads but none of them were Chelsea. It seems they never own up to the losses, so a bit of a result for the Gooners again.

Another story I have been told is of another 'off' at Anfield, by both sides – Liverpool and Chelsea. First the Chelsea version:

*We had about four hundred to five hundred lads off the train and knew there were more coming. No one was at the station to meet us, just a few Old Bill. We took the piss and decided to walk to Anfield, a good thirty-minute walk away, and let them know Chelsea were here. Close to the ground we came across a mob of about a hundred odd and steamed at them. They legged it and we gave chase and, nearer the ground, they vanished. We decided to meet up at the big park near the ground with other Chelsea lads who were coming up by coach. When we got there a big mob of Scousers clocked us and it was on. We went straight into them. We outnumbered them, and it was toe-to-toe stuff before they legged it, the weak Scouse c\*\*ts. Liverpool, they are shit. We took their manor and only Old Bill stopped us going on to the Kop. They were lucky that day.*

So Chelsea reckon they done Liverpool on home turf and outnumbered them, something I find hard to believe at Anfield. I have been there on the Kop and if Chelsea reckon they would have stood a chance on there they were kidding themselves.

The following is from a Scouse lad, about the same game:

*Fucking Cockney c\*\*ts came up here and tried to take the mick. We copped a massive load of them at Stanley [the park], and we ran at them. They did not want to know and there were only a few who fought because they were trapped. The rest legged it. The coppers were in it now and my mate got this Cockney c\*\*t's sheepie off him. He grabbed the lad [who] was in such a rush to get away he pulled the sheepie right off him. He was made up and still has it as far as I know. There was talk of the Cockneys going to get on the Kop. That would have been great, nowhere to run, we would have killed them again. Chelsea shit it bad that day and only seem to be any good when they are safe in the ground, behind Old Bill, or attacking small firms. We taught them a lesson that day.*

It seems they did meet up at the park and I would put my money on the Scousers as they were at home. The bullshit from the Chelsea lad about wanting to do the Kop – fuck me, you need a good firm to make a dent in it, let alone take it, so who would you believe? Anyone who has been to Liverpool will know what I mean, but they still claimed a result. It seems if three hundred to four hundred Chelsea lads turn up it's a result for them.

The story I like is about the FA Cup final against Leeds. I went to the Wembley one, but not the replay. In fact, I saw

Chelsea give Leeds a run for their money and in my eyes came out on top. Chelsea have had many a result against many an opposition, but to say they won them all is pushing it a bit far. Still, not many of their fans will own up to getting done. When they did they make excuses, saying, 'We got split up by Old Bill', or something similar.

Everyone has a story about Chelsea. Here is another from a West Ham supporter:

*I grew up in Grays, Essex in the mid-Seventies and, although it was West Ham, there were plenty of hard cases who supported Chelsea. It was a result of Chelsea's success on the pitch in the early Seventies. It seems a Cup win attracts the hangers-on, together with the fact Chelsea had not long been promoted from Division Two and were terrorising the country as they went. They even had a mob at the CBL at the Den – it filled me with dread going there. I knew West Ham were good but, what I heard about these boys, they were in a different class.*

*We played them away at Xmas 1977. Three of my mates and I decided, against our better judgement, that we would go on the Shed, more to boast to our mates that we had been on the Shed than anything. It carried a fearsome reputation and we weren't looking to get involved with anything. There was a bad atmosphere about the place.*

*Every Chelsea c\*\*t was seething and pointing to the middle of the terracing where, right in the middle, about three hundred to four hundred West Ham were standing. The Shed boys in the corner were giving it the large one and a massive Old Bill presence kept Chelsea up in the corner and West Ham where they were. West*

Ham were singing, 'We took the Shed.' We watched, as we were unable to join them as many were knocked back by Old Bill. I reckon there was another three hundred West Ham on there in scattered groups. The Old Bill had tried moving the West Ham lads down the front terracing, towards the pitch. This was Chelsea's cue to kick it off, as they said they would do. It seemed like a massive wave of Chelsea lads surged towards the West Ham lads from the Shed bit and a big roar went up and the West Ham lads ran at the Shed lads, who in turn had it on their toes; they did not want to know. This gave a load more West Ham time to join up and Old Bill kept moving us towards the front as the Shed was ours and they themselves weren't happy.

I have heard of coppers looking after their own fans and at Chelsea the only way they got the Shed back was because Old Bill shoved us off. It took them a while but they got us down the front again. Chelsea had another go and it was toe-to-toe stuff for a while and, when we rushed back at them again, they legged it. Some were chucking things at us. Old Bill finally got us on to the pitch and the Chelsea lot got their Shed back, but a few well-known faces demanded we have a go back again, once the Chelsea lads had the audacity to sing they had run us. We were well pissed off at that and back we went. Going uphill was a recipe for disaster, but fuck it, the Old Bill kept us back and we were escorted around to the North Stand to link up with many other West Ham lads. The truth is, if Old Bill had not moved us out we would have been there today. Never again did I bother with much respect for the slags. Every now and again I look at the paper cuttings. What a day, I was hooked for life.

I know, as many other lads will, about the feeling of being hooked for life. He also wrote about other run-ins with Chelsea:

*My next visit was two years later. We were both in Division Two. It was a night game, I think, and there was a bit of a rumble in the Shed. I dunno what went off as I was in the North Stand because I had got there late. After the game, on the way back to Fulham Broadway, Chelsea were swarming around and a big roar went up and they charged into about two hundred of us. It was not a good move. We were more than up for it and chased the fuckers all over the place, once they found out we were standing. They never had the bottle – the look on their faces was one of the funniest I have seen. It was a 'This don't happen to us' sorta look. I will never forget this one Chelsea spotty c\*\*t. He squealed and copped a good slapping, it was brilliant. They thought no one would dare do this on their manor but, for us, it was like a birthright.*

I have been in contact with a lad from Chelsea lad who was at this same game and he confirmed this story but he reckoned it was bad and we had about five hundred not two hundred. Still, it was a result for West Ham. He said he was only thirteen at the time and had never seen anything like it. He never doubted the West Ham lads again, he says, and would always like them in front of him in the ground so he can see where they are. So, if it was two hundred or five hundred, it seems Chelsea copped a good slapping on their manor from West Ham again. You won't find that written anywhere – they never get done, remember?

Here are a couple of stories about Stamford Bridge games, both from West Ham lads:

*Shed not running!!!!???? I went to the Xmas fixture around '76/'77 and was stood on the North Stand terracing. West Ham arrived on the Shed from the left-hand side and there must have been four hundred to five hundred that just marched in, up the steps and right into the middle of the Shed. Chelsea couldn't get out quick enough!!!*

*Then, as Old Bill tried to move West Ham on to the pitch and up the other end, Chelsea came back and tried to have it with the few West Ham lads that were getting outta the front of the stand. Suddenly the whole mob (who by this time were walking straight down the pitch towards where we stood, despite Old Bill trying to make them walk around the pitch) turned and ran back at them again. Chelsea scarpered!!*

And this from another lad who was younger at the time:

*I was fourteen at the time and in the seats with my mate, watching as the Shed evacuated as West Ham piled in from all sides. The bit I remember was when the West Ham were on the pitch and Old Bill was walking them up to the other end. It was funny to watch as no one walked around, but across the pitch. The few West Ham lads left at the back were set upon by Chelsea lads and the mob on the pitch turned and they ran back into the Shed. It was like the parting of the Red Sea. Never seen a mob run so fast.*

It seems the Shed had fallen again, but will Chelsea admit it? Will they fuck! One of my favourite stories is the one about the return leg at Upton Park when Old Bill were expecting trouble. The newspapers of the day reported this:

*LUNATICS BLAMED FOR SOCCER FLAME-UP*

*Police and football officials this week blamed 'lunatics' for West Ham's worst outbreak of soccer hooliganism this season. More than nine people were arrested during Saturday's match against Chelsea which saw a pitch invasion by fleeing Chelsea fans 49 minutes before the kick off. The trouble makers have been identified as West Ham supporters as they got into the ground area reserved for the visiting fans.*

*Their ruse foiled West Ham's attempts to segregate supporters by restricting Chelsea fans to entrance by voucher only. The system meant that the area set aside for Chelsea supporters – the South Bank – contained only about 300 spectators, the lowest number this season.*

*Police decided to let in about 500 supporters who turned up without vouchers, and they now believe they were West Ham fans disguised as Chelsea fans. West Ham secretary Eddie Chapman said, 'The police decided to let the fans in and we abide by their decision. They must have been West Ham fans though why the lunatics would want to start trouble with 3000 Chelsea fans against them is beyond me.'*

There's also a picture with the report, showing mounted police trying to clear the Chelsea fans off the pitch. Which makes me think that, if they knew the voucher system was in use for the South Bank only, why did they not try and take the North Bank when there were no vouchers needed? They had the numbers and it would have surely been a bit of payback for taking the Shed early on in the season. At least they could have had a go, but no, straight on to the South Bank, used their vouchers and all tucked up safe and protected by Old Bill (they thought), starting to giving it the large one again, but not for long it seems. West Ham came to them again but not so far this time and a mob of approximately five hundred attacked three thousand Chelsea lads, who in turn had it on their toes on to the pitch. If anyone wants a copy of that newspaper report, mail me. I will gladly send them a copy.

It seems Chelsea don't have much luck with West Ham and I believe they haven't changed much to this day. What more can I say except I hope the truth does hurt. They will never admit being 'caged in' at Plaistow bus garage in the Eighties, calling for help and the Old Bill, while the ICF was outside laughing. They had been chased down the Barking Road by an outnumbered ICF and tried to take refuge there. I'll bet you won't read that in any of their books.

Another time there was an arranged meet with the so-called 'Headhunters' – at the Burley pub. They never showed. Early before the match we were about one hundred and fifty-to two hundred-handed and took it to them – they stood for about ten seconds then had it away on their toes. Nothing much else, just a general piss-take on their manor and as usual they were a big let-down on our manor. It seems they have been turned over by nearly every London team, which doesn't surprise me.

The following is something sent to me by an old-school Chelsea fan:

> I've been reading some of your posts on the Internet. Mate, I am curious to where this utter hatred of CFC comes from? I am a lifelong Chelsea fan and, although on the day, we've probably gone toe to toe, there's been a few good seasons where I've been down Upton Park more than I have Stamford Bridge, we are from the same streets literally.

*Most proper Chelsea boys have the utmost respect for the old-school ICF because we acknowledge that you have given out more slaps than you have taken. Contrary to belief some of us do admit to getting done. Some of the Chelsea books even admit to Arsenal having taken the Shed in the 70s and Kingy's book faces up to the Hammers taking the Shed and Gate 13.*

*If you read some of my previous posts [under the name of Tea Bar and Arthur fucking Chelsea], hopefully you can read between the lines and see I am not a cyber twat. I've pointed out times when our boys have stood together (Chelsea v Millwall – the night after the Bristol game etc.).*

*I won't bore you with name dropping but suffice to say I've drunk and fought alongside some of your lads in the past.*

Later he continued:

*I know what you meant about these so-called hoolies. They think an off is smashing a few pint glasses and chasing a few scarfers down the road.*

*As for Parsons Green, spectacular as it was, anyone can break a few windows, I'd hardly call it a moment of glory (as most others would have us believe).*

*There never was a Headhunters until the press invented them. Then the morons started to call themselves the Headhunters and it all spiralled from there. Most lads know CFC had at least three to five different firms operating out of various parts of north London and east (yes east!) Essex and Kent etc. – it was rare days indeed for you to see the firms joined together (Cardiff/Millwall etc. being the exception).*

*All the real atmosphere has gone now with the all-seaters and 33 quid a ticket (I remember cracking though the turnstiles or jibbing over the wall in the good old days). Although we did have a tasty firm (tasty by today's standards anyway) out for West Ham at the Bridge last season, though nothing much happened (a few fat lips, grazed elbows, playground stuff really).*

*I agree with you we need to hold these new-age fuckers back from ruining our well-earned reputations.*

*Personally, though, I don't think the passion is there in the youth of today. They are all up each other's arses too much.*

WELL, FUCK ME! A Chelsea lad who knows the score and admits to a few things. Cheers for that, mate, you are a diamond and have gone a bit of the way to restoring a bit of faith in the proper Chelsea lads (I know there are many and have said this previously). I told him that I reckon Chelsea would be better off dropping a league along with Arsenal for a couple of seasons to clean out (in Chelsea's case) the King's Road mentality – then maybe the proper fans would get back. They soon cleared out in the mid-Seventies when they were down in the old Division Two. Crowds of around ten thousand to eleven thousand were the thing then; proper lads. Now, well, I think the Chelsea lad has summed it all up.

# CHAPTER TWENTY

# HILLSBOROUGH
# (WITH A TALE FROM A FOREST
# LAD WHO WAS THERE)

The events of the Hillsborough tragedy changed the game forever. That fateful day, when so many Liverpool fans died in a massive surge and crush on the Lepping Lane End, the blame was passed around. The hooligan fences were the main reason that people died, as fans were crushed against them. The South Yorkshire Police claimed it was because there were too many fans in there. Fucking brilliant. I wonder how many are detectives now? It did not take much working out, that. Some said it was the fault of police as they left the main gates open so people could get in before the kick-off.

Who was to blame? There were 96 fans dead and the game was going to change forever. In the wake of the tragedy there was loads of finger-pointing and a report was called for by the government.

The Taylor Report, as most know, introduced the all-seater ground and the removal of the fences at games along with other changes. In one report they thought they had solved the problem of the terrace culture. I could go on all day about this but I will go straight on to the Forest lad's story and you can draw your own conclusions. Like many, he has seen the game fucked by the corporate image. He says:

*The FA Cup semi-final we had been drawn against Liverpool for the second year running. I wanted to go again, so a trip to a ticket tout on Charing Cross Road just above Cambridge Road was once again on the cards. Having got my ticket, all I had to do was wait till April 15, 1989 and semi-final fever would be here.*

*The day came and I got to St Pancras early for the train up there. There was loads of fans from both sides at the station and Liverpool and Forest fans were made to queue up along with the Chelsea lads, who had to play Leicester and could get promoted. We were made to wait and queue up, unlike the decent law-abiding people who were allowed on the train.*

*Jimmy Hill drove through and we cheered the moment. Probably five hundred to a thousand lads all together despite their colours, chanting, 'Jimmy Hill, what a wanker, what a wanker.' As we waited for the train to come in I felt sorry for the poor bastard.*

*On the train my mate and I sat with two Scousers and played cards. I did not see any Chelsea lads on the train, they got off at Leicester. More about those tossers on the way back. We got to Sheffield and the usual story – Forest lads on one bus and the Scouse scum on the other. Loads of South Yorkshire's finest watching and we were bussed straight to the ground.*

*The flags hung out of the windows, and if you read this I apologise to you whoever you were, but you were a fat lass with the kids crossing the road taking your time. There must have been two decks shouting at you to hurry up, you fat bastard. I always remember her poor son's face. Oh well, in any war there are always innocent casualties and hopefully she lost some weight because of it.*

*We had the Spion Kop end, which was a great end for standing on. We were in there about 2pm. The Lepping Lane End was already full and our end was filling up. There were a few offs with stragglers but only mild stuff. This little group of Scousers were in this little standing section down at the bottom right of the Kop, but just behind the goals. The Scousers had an inflatable ball and were hitting it around. There must have been five to eight pairs of hands go up every time the ball came down, loads of singing and the ground was getting pretty well packed by 2.30.*

*From what I could see, the players came out then on to the pitch. We cheered our boys, Nigel Clough (you could never beat Des Walker), Steve Chettle, Neil Webb. Cloughie had once again built a team.*

*The singing continued and the end started to fill up fast now. All four cages at the Lepping Lane End were full. 3.00 pm came and kick-off about 3.07 I guess, but can't be sure. Beardsley hit the cross bar and the 'ooohhhh' went up. Down our end we weren't to know what some policemen had decided to do and I doubt they would have if Beardsley had not hit the woodwork. The roar would not have gone up, and the fans would have been still outside.*

*Anyway, first thing we noticed was some lads climbing over the cages. We thought, Typical Scouse, starting trouble again, especially after Heysel. Then a few ran down our end and started jeering at us. I hope you are proud now, lads.*

*For the next hour and thirty minutes events*

*unfolded, with fans ripping down advertising hoardings to carry their dying mates down to our end, where the ambulances waited. In the Forest end we had been told nothing at all. We were treated like scum and, in the eyes of South Yorkshire's finest, we were I guess. That was football in the '80s and early '90s. Even though you had paid ten quid for your rail ticket, at the end of the day you were still scum. Thanks, Mrs Thatcher, you were fucking great.*

*When the police finally let us out, they had closed the streets in town and pointed us up some fucking laneway. Fucking marvellous, walking through some shitty council estate in Sheffield without a fucking clue where you were going. Finally we found our way to the station and still had no idea what really occurred. Some Forest lad on the platform had a radio and he was telling us there were forty dead. We were still not really sure what happened. On the train information and gossip got passed around but other than that there was no one really interested apart from the football.*

*Then the Chelsea lads arrived back. We congratulated them on their promotion but let them know they would always be scumbags. I was always up for a piss-take, but that day it wasn't called for; but once a c\*\*t, always a c\*\*t.*

*Back at St Pancras, we had a few beers in a pub across the road and it still had not sunk in.*

*When the good and the great at the FA decided when the replay was on, we got our tickets and set off for Manchester. Well Alridge, you must be awfully proud, telling us how upset you were etc., etc., and I'm so pleased you managed to get over it so you could rub Brian Law's hair, sadly for us. Had we won that game* we would have been the villains and maybe a Liverpool v Everton final was fitting.

We got there a few years later, beating West Ham in the semis (that is another story) and we played the Yids and that was marred by the pie-eating, wife-beating idiot.

I had a few other experiences at Hillsborough. In 1985 the miners were on strike and the opening game of the season, Nottingham Forest v Sheffield Wednesday, their first game back after Howard and Wilkinson had got them promoted. We had Trevor Christie, who was now up front. Living in Doncaster, it was a short ride with me dad to go to the game. We paid our dues and went into the Lepping Lane End. The chants of 'Scum, scum, scab, scab' coming from the Wednesday fans were greeted with 'Arthur Scargill, what a wanker, what a wanker' and 'We've got jobs and you ain't.'

All was in a quite good banter, until a black geezer in a suit in the Forest end hurled a pie at a bunch of lads in the right-hand side (I think it's the main stand). All the Forest lads charged from the cages behind the goals, knocking my dad to the ground in their haste. There must have been two hundred lads in this little corner just going for it.

When the police turned up they got set upon by both sets of fans and it ended up on the pitch. It finally quietened down and the attention went back to the match.

At the station a makeover had been done and they had recreated a mini Beirut it seemed. A mate told me two Forest lads had been stabbed with strip lighting and running fights up and down the platforms *continued. Luckily, we hopped on a train to Doncaster and we were off. I've always been a lover, not a fighter.*

*The Hillsborough disaster left 96 dead and 400 injured and destroyed a lot of families' lives. In some ways it has destroyed what football meant to me. No more standing, no more real atmosphere at grounds any more. Sadly, the people who have made laws in football have never been to a game. Here is a message to you, Tony Blair. Just because you kicked a football with Kevin Keegan, it doesn't make you a Newcastle fan. You are going to make the same mistakes Thatcher did.*

*How you can stop 'suspected' people going abroad is beyond me and the British people have allowed a law that is pretty close to Nazi Germany go through. For a country that has prided itself on its liberty and freedom it's a disgrace.*

*Ever since British teams have travelled in Europe it seems to have been that the worst cases of trouble have been in Belgium. I wonder if maybe the country which brought us Maigret and Poirot has something to answer for when it comes to policing.*

*The Heysel disaster was a prime example of bad policing and segregation. The ECWC of '76 with the Hammers was also in Belgium and I am sure there are more cases.*

*Sadly our politicians have no understanding of football and the FSA have tried but failed because of the media. The lads who follow England are treated like scum wherever they go. Every little Johnny Foreigner wants to have a go and our boys don't back down.*

*I followed football between '84 and '92, which*

*wasn't like the golden age of the '70s, and what we have now is certainly a long way from a golden age. We have had something that is ours stolen from us by the money men, the politicians and the media men, and it's a shame. The comradeship I have had following Forest from London was fantastic and I loved it. I even managed to travel to Manchester on two consecutive weekends with the same ticket to see us against Man United. They lost 1-0 with Pallister scoring in the first game and I think it was 2-1 with Clough getting the winner the following week.*

*For me football wasn't about fighting, but it was a thin line. My mate who was with us, a postman from Muswell Hill, liked a ruck. Me? Like I say, I am a lover not a fighter, but the game has been stolen from us and we will never get it back, which is a shame.*

*I sat next to a young lad who is now a Leeds fan, and I could forgive him for not knowing who John Charles was but not knowing Trevor Cheery, Joe Jordan and Gordon McQueen – how can that be? All these new Man United fans today have probably got no idea who Paul McGrath, Norman Whiteside – let alone the Greenhoff brothers, Lou Macari and Pearson – were. It's all a shame that the history of football counts for fuck all. Maybe I'm an old c\*\*t but it's still a shame.*

Well, you have one real fan's view on how he feels about the game that we once owned. He goes a bit political for a while but all he says is true as far as I am concerned. In the old days, the Saturday afternoon game was only ever stopped because of the weather, not because of the TV men. The all-seater has fucked a way of life for many and, while they say it has stopped the fighting, it hasn't. It has only made the player more money because you now have to sit and spend a small fortune on a season ticket every year, just to watch your game.

# CHAPTER TWENTY-ONE

# MANCS (PART 1): THE GAME AT OLD TRAFFORD

A game that was to be held at the Theatre of Prawns, playing the underdogs West Ham, caught most West Ham fans' attention. Surely the Mancs would win, many said, just as they would win the FA Cup again. The Man United team had the arrogance to book their hotel in Cardiff to be ready for the FA Cup final. Ryan Giggs was even giving media interviews saying how great it would be to win the Cup in front of his home crowd – not *try* to win, but *win*!

On January 7, 2001 at about 6pm, the draw for the FA Cup, Fifth Round took place. A numbered ball was pulled out of the FA's draw machine and then came the words, 'Manchester United will play ...' The fans of the nation held their breath – whoever was called out next would surely be knocked out of the Cup. 'West Ham' was called out.

Many expected it to be a premature exit, but it was not to be. Little did Man United know that West Ham and their fans had other plans. This was the dream tie for them and a chance to shut up the Mancs once and for all. Many had vowed to never go back after a humiliating 7-1 loss the season before, but this tie caught the imagination of many and already groups of lads were plotting the trip up.

It was revealed that West Ham would get 9,000 tickets for the tie and when they went on sale they were quickly snapped up. The club offered free coach travel to its fans and rumours started going around that many an old face from the ICF days would make the trip. The last time these two clubs played in the FA Cup the attendance at Old Trafford was well down. In fact, many blamed the travelling ICF for this, such was the reputation they carried. Every other week Old Trafford was full, but for this FA Cup game it was well short of capacity and a touch over forty thousand attended.

I could do a book on its own about that game, but I've tried to pick the best tales. The first is the story of some lads travelling up to the game:

> *From the moment I met the coach, at Corly service station on the M6, I knew it was going to be a day to remember. With nine thousand-plus travelling up to Old Trafford, a place where we had lost in eleven successive visits, we went with hope, rather than expectation.*
>
> *As I crossed to the northbound side of the motorway the place was banged out with West Ham. The coaches laid on for free by the club, 128 in all, had started to arrive, and the place was awash with claret and blue. There were four Mancs braving the crowds who went into the services, only to be greeted by a rousing chorus of 'Who the fucking hell are you?', as they found themselves a quiet corner.*
>
> *Most had travelled up on the free coaches, yet there were many more independent travellers, like our-*

selves, who had hired their own. Some went up in stretch limos, while some old West Ham lads had four coaches taking them up there, complete with free bar and hostess service!

The Old Bill had everything pretty much under control, as they were meeting all the coaches, by now in full voice, off the motorway, and under escort to Old Trafford. On arrival we were guided to our parking spot, then left to walk the short journey to the ground. What came as a surprise was the lack of bodies around. Apart from a strong OB presence, there were few Mancs around as we made our way to the ground.

Now, I have been to Old Trafford many times in the past, although this was the first time I had gone there for about ten years, and I was struck by the way things have changed. It wasn't just the stadium itself, but the whole atmosphere has altered beyond all recognition. I can remember times when you could cut the air with a knife, such was the tension and hostility as you walked from Warwick Road, or from Piccadilly, but today, nothing, the place seemed sterile. There were more people in the merchandise shop than were milling about on the forecourt. Even the old boy who used to walk around with a sandwich board, proclaiming, 'The End of The World is Nigh', had disappeared, although by the end of the game it must have felt as though the world had indeed ended for some!

Entering the ground it was difficult not to be impressed by the sheer size of the stands, although it does look a bit like a patchwork quilt, as bits are added on here and there, in order to satisfy ticket demands, so that the ground seemed to lack the continuity of places like Sunderland's Stadium of Light.

It was the West Ham fans who brought the place to life, having the whole of the East Stand upper tier, as well as the section of the lower tier usually reserved for the away support. Chorus after chorus of 'Bubbles' went up, as we approached kick-off, bringing little or no response from the Red hordes. As the teams took the field there was a deafening roar, not dissimilar to the ones heard as you came out of the Wembley tunnel, as balloons and ticker-tape were thrown from the West Ham section. The cries of 'Come on you Irons!' went up, getting louder and louder, as West Ham started the brighter of the two sides. Fifteen minutes into the game, and with the Mancs starting to turn the screws, their supporters began to find their voices, and for the next twenty minutes or so things didn't look quite so good for the 9,000 of East London's finest, as West Ham were pushed back. However, after weathering the storm our voices had recovered, as 'Harry Redknapp's Claret and Blue Army' was belted out by all those present. All of a sudden it was the Mancs who went quiet, as they were held to a 0-0 scoreline at half-time. So quiet were they that West Ham began several choruses of 'Shall we sing a song for you?' at the break.

The half-time 'entertainment' consisted of an interview with some of the soap stars from Coronation Street, with the guy who plays Kevin Webster looking very unimpressed, as the cry of 'Who the fucking hell are you?' went up again from the travelling contingent, followed by the singing of the theme from rival soap EastEnders!

The best was yet to come for the visitors, as West Ham took control of the second half. Despite having a couple of reasonable chances, the Mancs simply couldn't get through the wall of claret-and-blue defenders. By now Joe Cole was on fire, with the ball at his feet, running at the Mancs' defence, and displaying all the tricks in his armoury. The West Ham fans could sense something special was going to happen as our voices drowned out all the Mancs could offer. A neat period of passing found Kanoute with the ball at his feet, with a flat defence in front of him. Paolo Di Canio made a run across the defence, as Kanoute slipped the ball through. Time seemed to stand still, as the Mancs appealed in vain for offside, with the linesman clearly leaving his flag down. Barthez tried to put off Di Canio, raising his hand in an effort to put him off, but the Italian genius simply stroked the ball home with the outside of his right boot. Cue 9,000 fans going fucking mental! Seats were broken, as you were being hugged by complete strangers, even kissed full on in some cases! There were a few tears, as even a hardened campaigner as myself was moved by the passion shown at that moment.

The last fifteen minutes, plus the four minutes' injury time, seemed an eternity, as we cheered, sang and chanted our way to a famous victory, which would make us the heroes of a nation – well, all except for Manc fans, and a scummy little piece of south-east London! The celebrations at the final whistle were as loud and long as I can ever *remember, as the Reds skulked out of Old Trafford. West Ham had won the day, and nothing was going to change that.*

*On the way out we were on our guard for anything that might go off, but once again a massive police presence ensured that things were under control. Despite the various threats that had been made to West Ham, there was nothing about, although the Mancs did claim to have a firm of five hundred plus in waiting, though nobody seemed to witness it. The old lads that went up hung around for a while, but met nobody, though the Mancs claimed it was West Ham that didn't show. Either way nobody can deny that the day was a complete piss-take from start to finish: to take that many to Old Trafford, beat probably the finest team in Europe, then turn the place into an Upton Park soundalike was amazing.*

*I'd like to finish by quoting a story confirmed by several different people who witnessed this event:*

*'Whilst walking across that little iron bridge outside the ground that many of the Mancs were threatening to hang themselves from ... suddenly came a charge of Mancs shouting, "They're West Ham, get them"... then after much kicking out at a rented van, smashing of lights and windows ... they suddenly all realised that the hired van contained a bloke in a bright red shirt with the name Beckham and a number 7 on it!'*

*They truly are some of the biggest wankers I have come across!*

So that's how one lad's day went. I think it says it all.

The following I picked up from the Mangler site and have used it with their kind permission – I thank them. A little poem that says it all really:

'*Fuck Man United and the Theatre of Dreams*
*Fuck what it stands for and all that it means*
*Fuck Sir Alex, Charlton and Best*
*Fuck the Red Devils and fuck all the rest*
*Fuck the K stand and fuck Busby Way*
*Fuck all their fans and all that they say*
*Fuck Sharp Electronics and fuck Reds Cola*
*Fuck I hope they all die of Ebola*
*Fuck Mr Beckham and fuck Giggs, fuck Keane*
*Fuck the most arrogant wankers that I have ever seen*
*Fuck the history and fuck their success*
*Fuck the trophy cabinet and the fact we have less*
*Fuck them all and their kids*
*Fuck the wankers they are worse than the Yids*
*Fuck the form book and don't get your head in a spin*
*We are going to go there and we are going to win!!!*'

I think that really sums them up. Many thanks to the Mangler site. These are sentiments endorsed by fans from many clubs, not just West Ham.

Back to the game. Talk of Man United fans giving the West Ham fans a hiding was heard. Some known Manc lads reckoned they would be out in force to do West Ham fans over, either at Trafford Bar station or Lou Macari's fish shop. The info was passed on by them to Greater Manchester Police but the police feared their manpower was already going to be overworked keeping the contents of the West Ham coaches under control. What makes me laugh is why mouth off they are going to do this or that, then let the Old

Bill know? Talk about covering your back and being scared! The so-called Red Army was already in retreat weeks before the game. Sound familiar? Why ambush fans at the train station knowing only a few would be on the train, when they knew full well nine thousand West Ham would be travelling up by coach. It's got me fucked. Just shows what cowardly c**ts they are!

I also got the following from the Mangler site and again many thanks for allowing me to use it and thanks to Ross – I think – for his work. He says:

*Dear one and all*

*I am happy to join you on Sunday at 2pm in what will go down in history as the greatest demonstration for freedom of our national game.*

*Five and five score years ago a great vision was realised and our great club was born and it is that majestic name that we will be defending on Sunday.*

*We are the great beacon of hope to millions of football fans who have been seared in the flames of the media's withering justice.*

*It will be as a joyous daybreak to end their long night of captivity.*

*However, one hundred and five years from our birth and we are no longer free. A century later the life of the football fan is still sadly crippled by the manacles of segregation and the chains of discrimination that everyday society has come to know as Manchester United Football Club.*

*One hundred years on the football fan lives on a lonely island of poverty in the midst of a vast ocean of material prosperity. One hundred years later the football fan is still languished in the corners of our society and finds himself an exile in his own land.*

*So on Sunday we go to dramatise and put right this shameful condition, in a sense we will go into the Hades that is Old Trafford to cash a cheque.*

*When the great architects of our past designed and then formed our beautiful game they were signing a promissory note to which every future generation of fans was to become the heir. This note was a promise that all supporters and teams will have an equal chance in the pursuit of happiness.*

*It is obvious today the Football Association and the media have defaulted on this promissory note in so far as the fans that refuse to support the red menace are concerned.*

*Instead of honouring this sacred obligations they have given the ordinary fan a bad cheque which has come back marked 'insufficient funds'.*

*But we refuse to believe that the bank of football justice is bankrupt, we refuse to believe there are insufficient funds in the great vaults of this nation. So we have come to cash this cheque, a cheque that will give us upon demand the riches of freedom and the security of justice in the face of corruption.*

*We will also go to Hades and remind the powers that be the fierce urgency of now. This is no time to engage in the luxury of cooling off or to take the tranquillising drug of gradualism.*

*Now is the time to make real the promises of equality, now is the time to rise from the dark and desolate valley of segregation to the sunlit path of justice.*

*Now is the time to lift our game from the quick-sands of injustice to the solid rock of football equality,* now is the time to make justice a reality for every one of God's football fans.

It would be fatal for the nation to overlook the urgency of the moment. This cold winter of discontent will not pass until there is an invigorating spring of freedom and equality

As we go into the first year of the new millennium, there is hope this is a new beginning.

Those who hope that the football fan needed to blow off steam and will now be content will have a rude awakening if things continue as business as usual.

There will neither be rest nor tranquillity in England until the football fan is granted his rights. The whirlwinds of revolt will continue to shake the foundations until the bright day of justice emerges.

But there is something that I must say to my people, who stand on the warm threshold that leads into the palace of justice. In the process of gaining our rightful place we must not be found guilty of wrongful deeds.

Let us not seek to satisfy our thirst for freedom by drinking from the cup of bitterness and hatred. We must ever conduct our struggle on the high plain of dignity and discipline.

We must not allow the performance of our magnificent team to go unnoticed as we degenerate into physical violence.

Again and again we must rise to the majestic heights of meeting their physical threat with our God-given voices and the power of our souls.

The marvellous militancy which is the travelling support of West Ham United will engulf their Hades. There is only one outcome.

*Many of us have passion overflowing in our hearts. It must not lead us into a total distrust of the media and the Football Association, for many of our opposing supporters at other clubs, as evidenced by their presence on our site, have come to realise that their destiny is tied with our destiny.*

*They have come to realise that their freedom is inextricably bound to our freedom. We cannot walk alone, and as we walk we must take the pledge that we shall always march ahead. We cannot turn back. There are those who are asking the devotees of the beautiful game: when will you be satisfied?*

*We can never be satisfied as long as the football fan is treated like the infidel in his own land, subjected to the propaganda and the false promise that is Manchester United Football Club.*

*We can never be satisfied while the referees treat the players of our clubs differently because of the colour of their shirt or the crest of their club.*

*We can never be satisfied while the child in a playground in the south has his mind polluted that his local side is void of worth while a child from the north is told that he has no opinion but to bow to peer pressure to support a team with which he has no ties.*

*We will not be satisfied while the parents of these children feel obliged to turn their backs on their roots for the sake of their children's future and status.*

*No, no, we are not satisfied and we will not be satisfied until justice rolls down like waters and the righteousness like a mighty stream.*

*I am not unmindful that some of you will arrive at Old Trafford after much trial and tribulation. Some of you have come fresh with the thought of New Year's*

*Day, some of you have come from areas where your quest for freedom left you battered by the storms of the red menace persecutions and staggered by the winds of media brutality.*

*You have been the veterans of creative suffering, continue to work with the faith that unearned suffering is redemptive. Know that when you go back to Upton Park, Stratford, Canning Town or to Barking, Dagenham, Romford or Hornchurch, those from the Ockendond and Avely, the Essex towns of Chelmsford and Colchester, those forced into relocation because of demographical change, those who are from further afield, go back to small houses and bad weather of our northern cities knowing that somehow this situation will be changed.*

*On Sunday we shall rise up from the valley of despair.*

*I still have a dream, it is a dream deeply rooted in every football fan's dream.*

*I have a dream that on Sunday we will rise up and live out the true meaning of football.*

*I have a dream that on Sunday in the red hills of Manchester, the brave players of West Ham United will be victorious in the very face of the devil himself.*

*I have a dream that on Sunday one united voice, so loud the followers of the red menace will think they are facing God himself on this judgement day, will be heard across this great land, singing the sweetest of melodies that only victory will allow.*

*I have a dream that our three children will boss the midfield and sweat blood while oozing character, showing an experience and hunger beyond their tender years.*

*I have a dream that the great Italian wizard will perform his magic, that the fantastic Frenchman will weave in and out of their defence like only he can.*

*That the defence will be like a rock upon which we can build our most glorious of victories.*

*I have a dream!!*

*I have a dream that the fans of Tottenham, Arsenal, Liverpool and Newcastle will shake our hands in eternal gratitude for stopping the red menace.*

*This is our hope, this is the faith that I will go north on Sunday morning.*

*With this faith we will be able to hew out of the mountain of despair a stone of hope. With this faith we will be able to transform the jangling discords of our nation into a beautiful symphony of brotherhood, knowing that by 4.00pm we will be free.*

*This will be the day when all of Harry's children will be able to sing with new meaning 'I'm Forever Blowing Bubbles'.*

*And so let the journey begin – From the coaches at the Boleyn, from the coaches at Barking station, from the train and the tube stations of London, from the garages of those who can afford them.*

*We do not come to just make up the numbers, we do not come just to be the whipping boys.*

*Let it be known in every hill and mountainside and in every town, village and hamlet across the land.*

*Let it be known that we are the same West Ham United who stopped them before from winning the Premiership crown.*

*We are today the very same West Ham United who*

*will put them out of the FA Cup and when it is done*
*and only when it is done we will be finally free at last,*
*free at last, free at last!!!*

So there you have just one lad's thoughts on how he, and I am sure how many of us, feels. Once again many thanks to the writer – T Ross, I think – and to Mangler site for allowing me to use it.

It is said that Man United fans were not happy at having such a large and noisy lot of fans attend their hallowed turf. Even the captain Roy Keane had a pop at his own fans, saying they were basically what many of us know them to be – fucking glory-hunting wankers who know fuck all of their team or the game. A media report from an interview with the Manc captain appeared and it went like this:

*KEANE SLAMS THE PRAWN EATERS*
*Manchester United captain Roy Keane has hit out*
*at sections of the Old Trafford support who he*
*claims can't even spell football, never mind*
*understand it. The Republic of Ireland international*
*admitted that he was frustrated by the poor*
*atmosphere at the Wednesday night Champions*
*League victory over Dynamo Kiev, a result which*
*secured the club's place in the second group phase of*
*the competition. 'Sometimes you wonder do they*
*understand the game of football,' said Keane 'We*
*were 1-0 up then there are two stray passes and they*
*are getting on players' backs, it's just not on. At the*
*end of the day they need to get behind the team.*
*Away from home our fans are fantastic, I'd call*
*them the hardcore fans, but at home they have a*
*few drinks and probably the prawn sandwiches and*

*they don't realise what's going on out on the pitch.'
Keane told MUTV, 'I don't think some of the people
who come to Old Trafford can spell football, never
mind understand it.'*

*His manager has also been at his diplomatic best
when recently describing some sections of the
support as crisp eaters more interested in their food
than the football.*

So there you have it. The captain and manager saying what
most of us already knew. Next time you have the
unfortunate experience of talking to a so-called Manc fan,
bring up the subject of football and ask who he follows.
Most will say they have been a fan since this day or that day
but most won't as they are the new-age, glory-hunting, no-
one-can-beat-us c\*\*ts; they are as simple as that. Even their
own mainstream fans know it and many hate them. But
who cares, they are all c\*\*ts anyway. Funny how the Man
City fans are not bad but the United ones are all gobby –
could never work that out. Goes with being a prat I would
say, unless someone could tell me otherwise.

On to the game. What you have read so far is just a warm-
up to the big event, the game itself and one lad's story on
how he felt:

*One of the strange things about the aftermath of this
match was the lack of match reports on websites, chat
forums and the like. I normally bang one out the day
after the game, but for this match I felt that I could
never do the event justice. For those who could not get
to the game and for those whose main link to the club
is the chat sites and email, someone should at least
try. With apologies to those who went for my failure*

*to capture the sheer magic and disbelief that was Sunday, January 27 2001, here goes.*

*Looking back at the build-up to the match, although I refused to acknowledge it at the time, an unstoppable irresistible momentum was built up by players, fans, even the directors of this club, that made the result a racing certainty. Think of how you felt when you first heard/saw the draw. Home team Manchester United – please not us, please not us – away team West Ham United – oh bollocks, we're outta the Cup!*

*How different was that feeling to the feeling you had when your alarm clock went off – oh my God o'clock on Sunday morning. From despair to 'I cannot wait for this match to start.' You can see how the whole thing built up, how your heart lifted as the match got nearer, when you found out that we would have 9,000 fans there.*

*All this was set against a match for which there was no logical credible way to reason that we could win. They were the better side in the country, they had a core of players who had been together for four to five years and won every honour in the game, they have a manager who has virtually eliminated complacency so that any fired-up underdog cannot rely on outworking them. We had not beaten them for nearly a decade, with eleven consecutive losses away, of which the last three were slaughters.*

*Against this Harry assembled his six million-odd-pounds' worth of the elderly, the mentally unstable, the unwanted, and a few boys asked to do a man's job. Most of the team had been first-team players for less than a year. We had a goalkeeper plucked from*

*Newcastle's reserves carrying an injury, we had two defenders in their late thirties who had lost their places at previous clubs, one who was not even allocated a squad number.*

*We had two loanees with less than a handful of Premiership games between them, one of whom came with the label 'phenomenally unstable'; the other defender was playing his second Hammers game fresh out of a First Division club reserves. The two strikers both came having fallen out with their clubs and were not playing for their teams at the time. The midfield facing the unchallenged might of Roy Keane and his gang were two 19-year-olds and a 22-year-old. Even Harry's staunchest supporters thought that taking on Keane and the rest with Cole, Carrick and Lampard was suicide; ditto playing Cole and Di Canio together and playing three at the back.*

*Sorry about the preamble but the sheer scale of the task has to be appreciated in order to understand the magnitude of victory. West Ham began with a 3-5-2 but with Kanoute playing on his own most of the time and Cole and Di Canio taking on a defensive burden to make the system more solid. Although we started under the cosh crucially we were competing strongly all over the pitch and harassing their midfield and working fully to cut off the supply to Beckham and Giggs. Hislop caused the biggest alarms with some highly dubious kicking and Giggs got free a couple of times but as the half neared its close, belief began to seep into the team and we began to move the ball though the midfield extremely well.*

*Off the pitch the visiting fans maintained a barrage of noise and sounded fantastic on the TV coverage so I am told. As half-time sounded Winterburn acknowledged the visiting support with a clenched fist, showing how important it was to reach this part of the game still very much in the match.*

*After half-time Man United took the game to West Ham for about five minutes but the youthful midfield really began to start playing. At times they bewildered Keane and Butt with some excellent passing and movement, my personal favourite being cornered-and-surrounded Cole by the flank releasing Kanoute with a sublime back heel. Kanoute himself began to twist and turn with the ball.*

*For twenty minutes we were the better team and when the goal came it was deserved. No need to describe the goal. We have all seen it. I remember it in slow motion. Despite the celebrations I kept expecting ref Gherkin to disallow the goal. These sorts of things don't happen to West Ham – hell, they don't happen to any visiting teams at Old Trafford. I was truly convinced.*

*When Man United took the kick-off, 9,000-odd West Ham fans went totally berserk running down the aisles and hugging total strangers, and other Hammers fans fell to the floor and blubbed their eyes out. After that it was a case of clinging on, relief and joy unbounded.*

*At the whistle we were kept in the ground for half an hour after the game. Most would have probably stayed anyway. The joy on the players' faces at the end was fantastic to see, all accompanied by the entirely predictable harassing of the ref and the catalogue of excuses from the losers.*

*It took two days to even begin to come down from the*

*emotion and joy of the day. To be the heroes of all football fans across the land was an incredible experience. It now only remains to place this day alongside those others that will be revered by generations of Hammers over the next few decades and to hope this is the start of a journey that ends in Cardiff.*

While there was hardly any trouble at the game, the West Ham fans had a field day taking the piss out of the Manc fans. There were many reports after the game and many songs that sprang up all over. I will cover that in the next section.

# CHAPTER TWENTY-TWO
# MANCS (PART 2): THE FA CUP

West Ham knocked out Man United from the FA Cup and the footballing world was shocked, mainly the suits and new-breed fans who thought that Man United were unbeatable. To many other fans of many other clubs in England it was sheer joy to see them out. As they were probably seen to be the hardest team to draw, a loss to them could only advance every other team's chances at having a shot at the Cup which has eluded so many teams over the years.

When the aftermath of the game settled down, the excuses started to come from the Mancs. I won't go into them but simply pass on what was said by them and others taking the piss outta them. We will start with the biggest whiner of all, the laughable Sir Alec Fergie. This report appeared on the Knees Up Mother Brown site, sent in by a listee whose name shall remain anonymous. It says:

> *Furious Man United manager in sensational attack on cheating West Ham star. Sir Alec Ferguson has launched a blistering attack on West Ham United's Paolo Di Canio after the forward scored the goal*

*that knocked Manchester United out of the FA Cup this Sunday.*

*Ferguson was beside himself with rage with the talented but temperamental Italian, telling football website 365.com Di Canio's behaviour was a disgrace to the game. 'Now I'm all for foreign players coming over here and improving the skill level, you only have to look at the impact Cantona made, but for a player to come to Old Trafford and score in the way he did is just ridiculous.'*

*The furious Scot continued, 'It was quite clear that Fabien Barthez and the defenders were signalling for offside. Di Canio saw Barthez with his hand in the air but totally ignored him and played on. Barthez had blatantly adjudged him to be offside but the player just carried on and scored. That's cheating, plain and simple and there's no place for it in the game.'*

*However Di Canio was not the only individual to feel the anger of Ferguson. The Manchester United manager had some harsh words for referee Paul Durkin and his assistants. 'I thought the referee had a very poor game, particularly with the penalty incident. At times it was like he did not know he was at Old Trafford. He completely ignored the defenders' signals for offside and his time keeping was just a joke. There was at least a couple of goals left when he blew up. I should imagine he won't be handling a game here again.'*

Also this piece started doing the rounds:

*ATTENTION ALL PREMIERSHIP CLUBS*
*Following the Old Trafford debacle yesterday an*

*emergency session of the committee has decreed the following rules to be implemented with immediate effect:*

*(1) Henceforth once a quorum of Manchester United players raise their hands, an offside decision SHALL be assured. A quorum in this instance is deemed to mean at least two (although we do reserve the right to RETROACTIVELY amend this rule should any one player so react).*

*(2) The previous ruling about no visiting team receiving penalty kicks at Old Trafford shall remain stringently in place, however it has not been resolved that – in the specific case of a Manchester United player only – any future award shall be based on where the upended player finally lands, not where the actual offence takes place.*

*(3) The referee shall allow reasonable time at the end of normal playing time (referred to as injury time) for the home team to win the match. Should Manchester United be in a leading position at the end of normal play the final whistle shall be blown forthwith. Should this not be the case the referee shall consult the Man United bench through a method of discreet ticktack and will not finalise the game until instructed to do so by the aforementioned bench.*

*(4) Blaming the state of the pitch is an entirely reasonable and plausible excuse which may be taken into account in the rescheduling of future adverse results. Unpalatable facts such as that this was the same pitch used on New Year's Day between same*

*teams or that four Premiership wins (out of five starts)
had been registered since start of December at Old
Trafford shall not be entertained.*

*(5) Finally it shall be entirely appropriate for any
match officials not observing any or all the above rules
to be sorted out in the players tunnel.*

*Furthermore we would like to express our extreme
displeasure with the match officials on Sunday – (a)
not having granted the initiative to anticipate rule #1
above and (b) not granting a penalty for ugly brother
No. 1's Olympic standard dive which took him
outside the box to close to the by-line (c) blatantly not
observing rule #3 above.*

So as you can see it was a good piss-take all round and
noticed by the whole football world. As much as Manchester
United would have liked to shrug off the loss, many were not
going to let it slip away so easily.

Loads of fans' songs came out about it. When Man United
played Sunderland next in the League, the Mackem fans were
singing 'Paolo Di Canio' to upset the Mancs. Here are a few
of the songs I like about that day:

(To the tune of 'The Hokey Cokey')
> *'He puts his right arm up*
> *His left arm down*
> *He looks at the linesman but the flag is down*
> *So Paolo sticks the ball in*
> *And the scum are out*
> *That's what its all about*
> *Ooooohhhhh Fabby Barthez*
> *Ooooohhhhh Fabby Barthez*

*Ooooohhhhh Fabby Barthez*
*He's bent arm stretched*
*C\*\*t, c\*\*t, c\*\*t.*

*He puts his right arm up*
*Linesman's flag is down*
*Paolo sticks it in*
*And the Mancs are one-nil down*
*They're outta the Cup*
*Because the goalie fucked up*
*That's how West Ham knocked them out, out, out.*
*Ooooohhhhhhhhh Fabby Barthez*
*[same chorus as above].'*

Many thanks to Dazza.

And this one to the tune of 'Knees Up Mother Brown':

'*Who ate all the prawns*
*Who ate all the prawns*
*You Manc bastards, you Manc bastards,*
*you ate all the prawns.'*

To the tune of 'Oh My Darling Clementine':

'*Here comes Paolo*
*Here comes Paolo*
*Fab Barthez, stick your arm up*
*Stick your arm up*
*Stick your arm up*
*You stupid c\*\*t it's in the net.'*

And this one I love, to the tune of 'Amore':

> *'If the Munichs get beat after trying to cheat*
> *It's Di Canio*
> *And when Man U get stitched and they all*
> *blame the pitch*
> *It's Di Canio*
> *When we make them look crap after springing*
> *their trap*
> *It's Di Canio*
> *When the wankers don't sink because their*
> *sipping their gin*
> *It's Di Canio*
> *When the ball's in the goal and it's Joey Cole*
> *It's Di Canio.'*

And another to the tune of the 'Aeroplane Song':

> *'Who's that standing on the goal line*
> *Who's that with his hand aloft*
> *It's that poxy short-arse*
> *Who gave West Ham a laugh*
> *As Paolo put the ball into the net.'*

And this one is quite good – thanks, Doddy, and many thanks to Paul:

> *'I hear thousands sing and see claret and blue*
> *West Ham in full flow*
> *For me and you*
> *And I think to myself, what a wonderful world*

*I see Paolo score*
*It's sheer delight*
*To all Man United fans*
*We say goodnight*
*And I think to myself*
*What a wonderful world*
*The Durkin blows his whistle*
*To tell us it's time*
*The joy on our faces*
*Our voices fill the sky*
*With the fans in the stan, dressed in claret and blue*
*I hear Barthez cry*
*Sir Alex moan*
*They never learn*
*Why they're hated so*
*And I think to myself, what a wonderful world*
*Yes I think to myself, what a wonderful world oh*
*yeahhhhhhhhhhhhhhh.'*

A couple more songs and rhymes that came out – fuck me, the lads are quick!

*'Of Barthez United are proud*
*And shout his name long and loud*
*But with Paolo approaching*
*He forgot all his coaching*
*And waved to the fans in the crowd.*

*The Manchester keeper is fab*
*And the games he plays never drab*
*But as Paolo broke through, he hadn't a clue*
*As he seemed to be hailing a cab.*

*When Paolo Di Canio got through*
*What does the French keeper do*
*Instead of a save it's a sort of a wave*
*Was he asking to go to the loo?*

*When Paolo scored with such skill*
*He gave the whole nation a thrill*
*Man U were upset*
*When the ball hit the net*
*So next year they can go to Brazil.'*

The next one is a poem from the In The Know site and I thank Abbo for it. Well, done mate, it really sums up how most of us feel:

*'My name's Fabien Barthez, I'm a bald-headed frog*
*I am a shit keeper and a proper French knob*
*I think I'm shit hot, always taking the Michael*
*But I know I will be never be as good as Peter*
*Schmeichel.*

*My name's Phil Neville, I'm a loud-mouthed wank*
*My footballing skills aren't worth a wank*
*A well cocky bastard and an ugly one at that*
*I play for Man United and I'm also a twat.*

*My name's Wes Brown "wot 'appenin' brother"*
*I'm not quite black but a very strange colour*
*I can't find a bird with less than four holes*
*Perhaps that's why I only score own goals.*

*My name's Roy Keane and I think I'm well hard*
*Basically a gypo who likes the red card*

> *A big-headed Paddy always giving it to the ref*
> *I must be a prime suspect for the UVF.*
>
> *My name's Ryan Giggs with a head full of curls*
> *At school I got battered by all the girls*
> *A bit off a show-off and I think I'm quite pretty*
> *I'm too good for these clowns I should be at Man City.*
>
> *My name's David Beckham I'm sure you've heard*
> *I've got a stick insect that I call my bird*
> *I've got a big head and a dick like a maggot*
> *The rumours are true I am a red raving faggot.*
>
> *My name's Luke Chadwick I can play up front*
> *But have you ever seen a more ugly c\*\*t*
> *I'm riddled with acne but it might be the pox*
> *I could eat a roast dinner through my mum's*
> *letterbox.'*

Pretty well sums them up, doesn't it? The next one I like just as much. Again off the In The Know site – I have no name for the lad, but many thanks anyway. It follows to the tune of 'The Whole World in His Hands':

> *'We got fans in China and Zimbabwe*
> *We got Cockney Reds from Bermondsey*
> *We change our kit every week*
> *Because United are a PLC.*
>
> *We're the biggest club apart from another three*
> *We're being ripped off but we can't see*
> *Everyone takes the piss outta me*
> *Coz United are a PLC.*

*We dropped out of the FA Cup*
*We went to Brazil but not much luck*
*We get kicked out if we stand up*
*Coz United are a PLC.*

*We've named Warwick Road after Matt Busby*
*We watch them on the telly with a prawn sarnie*
*We've got our own channel on Sky TV*
*Coz United are a PLC.*

*We've got the hardest mob in the Premier League*
*With Cockneys and Taffies and the local Old Bill*
*Coz United are a PLC.*

*The club's in Salford in the heart of Lancs*
*But we're not so proud so we call ourselves Mancs*
*The board keeps the money in a London bank*
*Coz United are a PLC.*

*The clock doesn't work outside our ground*
*We go out in Knutsford and we call it town*
*And the goon Terry Christian says we're sound*
*Coz United are a PLC.*

*We've got Man U cola in our half-time shop*
*We get crowds of ten thousand if we're not top*
*Someone should repair that fucking clock*
*Because United are a PLC.*

*We've got kung-fu Eric, we call him God*
*We got eighty thousand players in the England squad*
*There's a shit Scottish singer and he's called Rod*
*Coz United are a PLC.*

*We had a rat-nosed keeper in a bacon ad*
*We sing Status Quo – how fucking sad*
*We're ripping off children in Baghdad*
*Coz United are a PLC.*

*We've got a number seven who wears a thong*
*His wife thinks he's top coz he talks like a mong*
*We listen to City and we nick their songs*
*Coz United are a PLC.'*

Again, just about sums them red c\*\*ts up – what do you think? In fact, if the nickname was not the Red Devils I bet it would be changed every few weeks to accommodate a new range of playing strips, which the stupid inbred fans would buy.

Back to the game.

As the West Ham fans were kept back after the game, a right piss-take started and the excuses from the Mancs came out. What really pissed off a lot of their fans and added further insult to injury was that about two hundred and fifty-odd West Ham old faces had hats made up and proudly wore them with the caption 'ICF 1975 – 1985 Undisputed Champions'. That went down a right treat I am told!

Other things happened after the match. One report was about David 'I'm too sexy for my shirt' Beckham, the England captain (what a fucking joke that is). Another about a car bomb outside the ground so the game should have been replayed. Dunno what would have happened if the Munichs won. The classic story was the moan about the pitch from the c\*\*t of all moaners, the fucking inbred Jock, who I am told loves fish and chips. What a fucking prize prat, to carry on like that. Being a Jock you should accept defeat from the English. I mean, it's not the first time and I doubt the last. More stories came out – one about the now England captain who allegedly spat at a West Ham youngster in his dad's car, who was taking the piss outta the player's team. Stories about it appeared all over the place, but the one I liked went as follows:

*THAT BECKHAM SPITTING INCIDENT –*
*THE TRUTH*

*West Ham supporter (name withheld) is claiming David Beckham spat in his face after he jokingly taunted the England captain in a traffic jam following the Hammers' FA Cup win at Old Trafford – and a DNA test will prove it. Becks however insists he is blameless over the gob-fuelled confrontation which occurred as their cars drew level on the way back from Sunday's game, and he may well have been. So what's the truth? Here are some possible explanations for what is known as 'spitter gate'.*

*1) David was merely illustrating how close chum Gary Neville spat his dummy during an angry confrontation with Paul Durkin following the referee's disgraceful decision to allow a perfectly good goal for the opposition at Old Trafford. He may have been illustrating how incredulous journalists spat out their treble whiskies as Sir Alex Ferguson painstakingly explained how November's Rugby League World Cup final was directly responsible for United's late January defeat.*

*2) Years of rooming with Stuart Pearce on England's get-togethers have converted David to punk rock. Tragically, the person's car drew level with Beckham's vehicle just as Posh Spice slipped* Never Mind The

Bollocks Here's The Sex Pistols *into the CD player and our hero showed his appreciation in time-honoured style.*

*3) A sudden attack of diarrhoea caused by playing on a bumpy pitch in bright Brazilian sunshine caused David to kawk out a loogie immediately. He did not notice the other person's car in the way since the other motorist was wearing a grey shirt, which rendered him completely invisible.*

*4) Fate, via a freak gust of wind, intervened just as Becks was using the traditional spit and polish method to clean the lenses of the Police sunglasses he is now promoting in exchange for a mere one million a year, or perhaps he was merely taking part in test shots for upcoming OK! cover feature: David's and Victoria's bodily fluids, a 24-picture special you will treasure forever.*

*5) Devotees of what is being dubbed as the magic spittle theory believe Beckham's phlegm travelled through his oesophagus and into his handkerchief then changed direction and passed through the exhaust pipe of his jeep, rebounding through the windscreen of the other person's car.*

So Becks chucks a wobbler – haven't seen him do that before, have we? I dunno how he will go after football! Rumours around say he will join Posh as a singing duo. Another Sony and Cher. Or take up Andy Gray's job as head Sky commentator so he could *really* talk about Man United and let the world know how great they are – something that Andy and his sidekick don't do enough of! Time will tell.

One moment that stuck out and will be remembered by fans all over the world is the goal as West Ham beat the offside trap and Di Canio scored. Barthez their keeper raised his hand to tell Di Canio it's offside and he must stop because he is a Man United player and therefore what he says is law (well, that's what Fergie told him). But Di Canio has always been a rebel and doesn't speak French, so fuck it, he scored it! The sheer horror of the Manc fans – how dare he, when the defenders and the goalkeeper said it was offside! This was not on, and Barthez's raised hand was a waste of time unless he was hailing a cab to beat the sudden departure of Manc fans from the ground knowing they would lose. He wanted to get away early. Bad luck, Barthez. I would play cards with you any time – poker would be a good game! I am actually surprised that Man United never called for their red shirt to be scrapped because they lost!

Reports of a car bomb outside the ground – and a controlled explosion carried out by police to see if it was real – were found out to be true, and many Mancs said the game should have been stopped because of the danger to the public; a replay was called for by some. Fuck me, if the Man United fans just owned up and said they were beaten by a better side on the day, instead of coming up with all this shite all the time, they might get a tiny – and I say tiny – bit of respect. The next story is about the pitch and Fergie's so-called chat with *Red Fanzine*. I thank *Red Issue*.

### FERGIE ON PITCH SOLUTION

*I had a meeting with Keith Kent about the pitch yesterday but we are up against it really. Other than having to re-turf the whole lot like last year, I am not sure what we can do. It is too late in the day to re-turf it all. If we did that and then got a downpour we would be in trouble.*

*The pitch is struggling. The way we pass the ball we need a good surface. We have to get our thinking caps on and see what we can do about it. We have known since the start of December that there was a problem beginning again. It was staring to move under the players' feet when they were doing the warm-up. We were getting feedback from them about it at the Tottenham game on December the 2nd. When it starts moving under their feet, that's when it is starting to break up.*

*The first signs that it was getting worse in a game came in the next few matches. A few weeks later against Liverpool the ball wasn't running true. It was bobbling and all of a sudden the players are fighting the ball. We had a lot of rain around October and November, an unusual amount, but there is no doubt that the rugby does not help. The club has to look at that but for the moment we have to get our heads together and decide what we can do to improve things.*

Fuck me, where did all his so-called superstars learn to kick a ball – on a giant-sized snooker table? What a load of bollocks. They had no trouble beating West Ham 3-1 a few weeks before. Funny, lose in the Cup and it's blame the pitch! That's why we won and why Liverpool beat them. Maybe that's why Barthez was raising his hand – to signal the pitch is not kosher and Di Canio should stop. If there's an excuse that Fergie can give to his glory-hunting c\*\*ts of followers he will find it. One moment he says they are not loud enough, the next he feeds them this bollocks and they swallow it. If for once in their lives they said they were beaten by a better side on the day, who knows, the rest of the football world might lay off them a bit – but I doubt it.

To put the icing on the cake, a few weeks later Fergie told reporter Ian McGarry the following:

> *Sir Alec Ferguson fears that Manchester United's dominance of domestic football could be damaging their chances of European success. A disappointing 1-1 draw at Old Trafford with Panathinaikos on Wednesday night has left the Old Trafford manager examining reasons for his team's lacklustre performance. With the Premiership all but wrapped up with nine games to play, and no FA Cup to compete in, Ferguson conceded that his team's edge might have been blunted by lack of real competition.*
>
> *He said, 'It's possible that the edge has been taken off our play because we are in such a comfort zone in the League. It's a concern for us but awareness of that is a key factor in remedying it.'*
>
> *No doubt Ferguson will also be conscious of the fact that, when United beat Bayern Munich 2-1 to win the European Cup two seasons ago, Arsenal pursued them in the title race until the final day and their 2-0 FA Cup final victory over Newcastle came four days before their Champions League success.*
>
> *There will be no repeat of that natural momentum this season and, in fact, United could struggle to find the necessary impetus.*

Have you ever heard so much shite in your life! Arrogance at its best. He now thinks his side is too good for the English Prem. The sooner they fuck off and take their arsehole players and so-called fans with them the better the game will be.

*SIGNS YOU HAVE BEEN IN MANCHESTER TOO LONG*

1. *You go mad when someone from Manchester says 'mad ferit'. 'Nobody ever says that ever,' you scream.*
2. *You say 'mad ferit' when back in Manchester.*
3. *You think fishermen's hats are attractive.*
4. *You support Man City out of principle.*
5. *You see* Coronation Street *stars all the time and think nothing of it.*
6. *You get a freckle and consider yourself suntanned.*
7. *You deny that it rains all the time – as you struggle home with the shopping in yet another torrential downpour.*
8. *You think Londoners are soft southern twats until they kick your head in at a football match.*
9. *You won't pay more than £1.50 for a wrap of skag.*
10. *People start yawning when you talk about how great Manchester is.*

FUCK OFF MANCHESTER UNITED, YOU ARE NOT WANTED – SIMPLE.

# CHAPTER TWENTY-THREE
# THE NEW GAME TODAY
# (WHERE'S THE OLD ONE?)

The game today has changed so much, it's hard to believe. Older fans like myself who have seen the changes from afar can only shake their heads. It must be worse for those still wanting to follow their teams but who cannot afford the outrageous prices imposed by their clubs. What was once an affordable game for the working class is now a media circus designed around the media moguls' greed to cover the games when they think the TV rating will draw the most money for advertising, and so on.

Some blame the massive wage bill for players. I reckon if people are making money out of you then why not be paid accordingly? The media moguls are not exactly earning peanuts, are they? While they pay up big money for TV rights, the players want a share. Although it's big money in the normal fan's eye, it is really nothing to the barons who run our game. They make the money back threefold and if they lose it's all a tax deduction for most companies. You never see them backing off when it comes around to renewing the coverage rights. Soon the game will go global – this has been covered in another book, Dougie Brimson's *Capitol Punishment*. It explains it quite well.

What, then, of the fans? Can you imagine an all-London team playing an all-Paris team and the fans that would follow them? The English hate the French and vice versa. If the authorities think there won't be trouble they are wrong. No doubt the English fans will be to blame – as proven in Euro 2000 by biased Belgian authorities.

The football fan travelling abroad is now guilty till proven guilty (mainly because he is English) in the eyes of Europeans, and the Blair government hasn't done much to help. Jack Straw introduced the Football Act but the Act may well be illegal under human rights legislation.

The Act is the Blair government's response to the violence at Euro 2000, the same knee-jerk reaction that saw shooters lose a lot of their rights and the handing-in of pistols to totally ban the sport after the Dunblane massacre. They thought it would stop a lot of the armed violence in the UK but, as the old saying goes, outlaw guns and only outlaws will have guns. They made honest people criminals because they liked to shoot at paper targets, while the police showed their slackness by failing to detect the Dunblane killer's past history and by issuing him with a firearms permit. Another cover-up.

I know this has nothing to do with football, but see the resemblance? If you are a football fan then you must be a hooligan, simple, and therefore guilty and you can have your passport taken away because the police may suspect you of being one. Does that mean all people with cropped hair are skinheads, or people who wear leather coats are Hell's Angels? It is so fucking stupid. It just ruins the game even more.

OK, some will say they are glad the football violence has quietened down, but that is mainly because of the all-seater and the police's new powers of detection, not because all of a sudden in this new-age world North likes South and vice versa. The people who are glad are probably the same ones giving it the large one at the game in the safety of his/her seat knowing help is not far away and who like to get on Internet sites and again large it up. I think you know what I mean. I doubt if the good old days (well, they were for me) can ever be recreated, but I don't think many would want that anyway. With the loss of those days, though, a culture has died.

There are still rival 'offs' between opposing fans. Maybe not as big as before, but better planned, through technology. The swaying has gone, the lads you knew are not there and the few who are cannot afford every game; it's just not the same. I watch West Ham on the TV and I see the old North Bank gone and the new stand in its place with nearly all away fans in it. I think, fuck that, what happened? That small piece of steel and concrete meant so much to me and many others and I, along with thousands of other Irons fans, have fought to keep it – but it means nothing now. The new fan only knows he can slag someone off from the safety of the all-seater. He would not have lasted on the terraces before the all-seater, but he is there now. With the introduction of a Euro Super League (God, I hope it never happens), competitions like the FA Cup, the oldest club competition in the world, will be only a minnow in the football world. We have already seen the Mancs snub it and go halfway around the world in search of a Mickey Mouse cup – and lose. Supposedly, they did it to help England's bid for the World Cup. What a load of bollocks! Their manager had no intention of helping England's bid (Scotland's maybe, but they don't count). He was there, along with the players who thought they were some kind of massive superstars, and snubbed the people. When the people there snubbed them back they changed their ways and all of a sudden were friendly. If I had my way the Mancs would be barred for at least ten years from the FA Cup – but that's me.

The new age has turned away fans who followed their teams all over, fans who knew their club history, who was the first manager, who was highest goal scorer and so on. The new breed of fan does not know this. He knows it's OK to wear a Man United or Arsenal shirt because they are two of the better teams and it's fashionable to be seen wearing them and easily changed if the team does no good. Over here in Oz, I know many Aussie lads who wear shirts from Man United, Arsenal, Chelsea and have added Leeds to the stable because of players like Viduka and Kewell (since departed for Anfield, of course) who are Aussies – well, sorta! Ask any young fan here whose parents are Croatian who he follows in the Prem and nine times outta ten it's Leeds because they have Viduka and he is Croatian. It makes me laugh. I know a few Greeks who liked West Ham because Stan Lazaridis played for us, and so it goes on. A lot of football fans now have an allegiance to the foreign players, who by most standards are overpriced, playing in what was once a British working-class game. Now they are sitting in the all-seater sipping their gins and munching on prawn sarnies and singing along because it's trendy to do so, wearing their replica shirt because it's the fashion along with a 'do-I-have-the-right-one-on-today?-Have-the-club-changed-it-from-last-week?' attitude.

No, the game's fucked. Just look at the crowds at games. Take my own team West Ham at Sunderland in the FA Cup. I couldn't believe the number of empty seats in the ground. I am told by Sunderland lads that it's because West Ham fixed the prices and it was too dear. I am also told that's not the case, by West Ham fans, but – no matter why – the tickets were too dear, simple. West Ham did it again with the Intertoto Cup, thinking they were into Europe again and they could charge sky-high prices, but it backfired and only about ten thousand fronted the next Toto game. They halved the cost and nearly got a full house. The true fans are not idiots. While I like satellite TV because I can now watch the games from over here, if I still lived in England I doubt that I would be able to take my son along every week to West Ham because of the prices. Something will give one day and it will be sooner rather than later.

What's good for the fans must be good for the players, the people most fans love and adore. Let's take Beckham. He gives a one-fingered salute to a section of the crowd because of some piss-taking, no problem. If a fan did that he would get barred, as did a lad from a Man City/Man United derby. He got barred for three years for doing the same and he wasn't even a hooligan. One rule for them, one for us.

While Blair's government has done its best to label all football fans as thugs, at the same time he is letting many convicted terrorists in Ireland go free. People who have bombed, maimed and killed go free, with no more than a slap on the wrist. It's got me fucked. To cap this all off, while the national stadium is being rebuilt a decision has been made to move the FA Cup final, along with the League Cup, to Cardiff of all places. Is Cardiff, of all places, really the only ground large enough to hold it? If we are going to move the English FA Cup into another country, why not go to Hampden, which we all know can handle the big games. Even Old Trafford now the Mancs are out (and should be thrown out for ever more because of the Brazil debacle). I mean, they can hold the north London semi-final there, so why not the final? At least it's in England – well, sorta.

# CHAPTER TWENTY-FOUR
# THE TRIALS AND TRIBULATIONS OF A HAMMERS FAN ABROAD – THE STORY OF BOBBI THE MOD FROM CANADA

Living thousands of miles away from the one you love is not the easiest thing in the world to deal with. I should know: West Ham and I have been apart for nine years now and it doesn't get any easier. When I say apart, I mean that week-in-week-out kind of marital bliss that all of you reading right now can relate to; the ups and downs, the whole stress factor that comes with travelling up and down the country for the cause. Endless excuses for why work must understand the need for you to be away on a Monday afternoon while you travel up north with your mates to watch your love mercilessly beaten into the ground.

With the advent of the Internet and cable television it is now possible for people like me to listen or watch all Hammers games from abroad, intermittently interrupted by mad dashes across the Atlantic to get the match-day experience at least three times a year, and sometimes taking in four games in a two-week period thanks to the nidge contingent. My ex-girlfriend even got so tied up in her love for West Ham that she left the cosmopolitan city of Toronto to go and work near Brighton to be nearer Upton Park than me and to prove that she's just as mad as I am, gawd bless her.

There's nothing quite like match day in east London. Catch the tube to Barking, swift pints and witty repartee in the Barking Dog out on the patio, visits to the bog to 'freshen up', to keep up with all the slang I've missed out on over the years, pretend I know what they are all talking about and keep a close eye on the new fashions that always seem to be born on the football terraces, even though I'm always one step ahead in that department anyway!

After a short tube ride to Upton Park it really begins to sink in: 'Who's playing?'; 'Who's injured?'; 'Is Cass still selling his wares up the street?'; 'Does pint-sized Doddy still read his fanzine from cover to cover outside before kick-off?'; 'Is Sukh still trying to out-dress me?' … all the questions hit me as I walk up Green Street. And have you noticed how much prettier the girls are on match day? Just an observation.

As Upton Park is approached, visiting fans tread warily towards their provided sanctuary and home for the next ninety minutes. All the while a twitch in me harks for the old days when you would never just let them walk by without some sort of comment or slap. It seems just a raised eyebrow of contempt is enough these days – that will change in the Nationwide, believe me.

Somehow West Ham never seem to disappoint when it comes to throwing away leads right at the very end of the game. It almost becomes an accepted part of life that when we are 1-0 up with five minutes to go we mange to scrape a draw. Same old West Ham.

After the game, which seems to last all of ten minutes, it's back to the Prince of Wales (RIP) and the ol' tin-of-sardines experience while trying to chat over a 300-decibel mixture of Madness, Cockney Rejects and the Beat while trying to lip-read the sports presenter on Sky Sports. All your senses have to be alive for this experience, which has now moved on to other pubs around the ground, none of which have the history and charm of the much-missed POW.

Watching a game in a pub here in Toronto, namely the Duke of Gloucester on the world's longest street (Yonge), is a completely different experience, obviously, with all the ex-pats that have been here as long – or longer – than I have, still stuck in the Seventies and Eighties; and it is not uncommon to be involved in a little dance now and then with the Spurs mob – keeps you sharp. There are even small Millwall, Chelsea, Blackburn, Leeds etc. crews that meet there for the live Sky games on Sunday mornings. Obviously the Millwall lot will never see their team on Sky on Sunday mornings, but they watch and learn, watch and learn. Then you have the Man United and Arsenal fans. Now I've tried to refrain from using the vernacular for this piece but I'm afraid now is the time to let loose. I've lost count of how many times some Canadian has told me that West Ham sucks and that I should support a good team like Man United. Just two evenings ago I wrapped a pool cue around some fucking muppet claiming to be an Arsenal fan while 1) never having been to a game in his life, 2) never having left Canada, and 3) telling ME how my team sucks. Several occurrences of this nature have been had here and I can happily report that word is slowly going round that West Ham are not to be messed with – witness the geezer in a nightclub who left the building through the fire exit door still sitting in his chair after making a schoolboy comment about my team while I was taking a piss in the bog.

Being so far away hasn't dampened my passion one bit. If anything, I believe it makes you more and more passionate as time goes on and nothing anyone can say to me will test my loyalty, be it the South African who delivers pizza (clocked him for taking the piss out of my Hammers doormat) or the post office clerk who is due an over-the-counter windmill for all the typical Man United bollocks he feeds me with every week – muppet!

The trials and tribulations of a Hammers fan abroad.

# RETIRE BOBBY MOORE'S NUMBER SIX

A campaign has been launched to have West Ham United's famous number six shirt retired as a tribute to England captain Bobby Moore, who died from cancer in 1993. This is not the first time a football club has retired a shirt in honour of a player's service: Italian club AC Milan did it to honour their long-serving defender Franco Baresi. We feel that Bobby deserves nothing less and that West Ham United should agree to do the same. This gesture would be a permanent reminder of Bobby Moore's greatness, especially if, in the West Ham United squad listings in match programmes, the number six was listed as 'Retired in honour of Bobby Moore OBE'.

Bobby Moore was the captain of West Ham across three decades. He wore the number six shirt for over fifteen years at Upton Park, playing a total of 642 times for the Hammers. He achieved the incredible record of 108 caps for an England outfield player, ninety of them as captain, and lifted the World Cup in 1966 – the only Englishman to do so in the history of the game. Moore was simply the best defender the world has ever seen. He was calm and skilful and his passing was phenomenally accurate. His positional play and ability to read the game bordered on the clairvoyant. Aside from hundreds of great performances for West Ham, his display against the Brazilians in the 1970 World Cup was so fantastic that at the end of the game the great Pele declined all offers to swap shirts with anyone except Bobby.

During Bobby's West Ham career he won the FA Cup in 1964 and the European Cup Winners Cup in 1965. He received the Player of the Tournament award in the 1966 World Cup and was also awarded the OBE in 1967.

This campaign has the full support of Bobby's wife Stephanie Moore, who has said: 'I think the campaign to have the number six shirt retired at West Ham as a tribute to Bobby is a wonderful idea. I am in complete agreement.'

Moore's great friend singer Kenny Lynch OBE said: 'Anything that keeps Moore's legend alive gets my vote.'

Capital Radio's Tony Gale, who played in Moore's number six shirt at both Fulham and West Ham, said: 'If anyone deserves the honour of having a shirt retired in their name, it's Moore. It's a gesture which would be very fitting.'

For further information about the Retire the Number Six campaign, contact Jon Vinton on 01934 522703 or email on: noj@westhamunited-fc.com, or alternatively write to him at 2 Gradwell Close, Worle, Weston Super Mare, Somerset BS22 7UZ, England.


BobbyMooreOnline.co.uk
Tribute site to West Ham and England's greatest player.

# THE SONGS

Some of the songs and chants of the times were a laugh. I can't remember them all, as there were so many, but I have jotted down a few I did like. I feel some of the chants set the scene or the mood of a game on the terrace and, while most times they were a piss-take, many intimidated the other team's fans – via a chant of 'You're going home in a West Ham ambulance' and so forth. The songs and chants really were part of – indeed, helped create – the atmosphere at a game. It always amazed me how quickly someone would think up the words for something relevant to the moment.

Chelsea came out with some good ones and I'll start with them, but as always Chelsea were better at singing than anything else.

To the tune of 'Smoke Gets in Your Eyes':

> *'They asked me how I knew*
> *Chivers was a Jew*
> *I of course replied*

"*His nose is much too wide
It should be circumcised.*"'

And another Chelsea one, to the tune of 'Glory Glory':

'*My eyes have seen the glory of the Yids of White
Hart Lane
We gave them all a kicking and left them there in
pain
We took the Paxton Road End and the Park Lane
and the Shelf
And the Yids go marching out, out, out.*'

Some for the Old Bill, the first to the tune of 'Campdown Races' and about a TV show of the time called *Dixon of Dock Green*:

'*Who's that fella with the helmet on?
Dixon, Dixon
Who's that fella with the helmet on?
Dixon is his name
On the beer all day, on the wife all night
Who's that fella with the helmet on? Dixon is
his name.*'

And this little one about Harry Roberts, the infamous villain who shot and killed two or three coppers at Shepherd's Bush in the mid-Sixties:

[sung to *London Bridge is Falling Down*]
'*Harry Roberts is our friend, is our friend, is our friend
Harry Roberts is our friend,
He kills coppers.*'

Some songs at West Ham which were popular at most grounds:

To the tune of 'Hey Jude':

> *'La la la la-la-la-la,*
> *La-la-la-la, West Ham.'*

This song went on for a fair while and was great to hear. To the tune of 'Distant Drums':

> *'I hear the sound*
> *Of distant bums*
> [Crowd points to away fans with a waving motion]
> *Over there, over there*
> *And do they smell*
> *Like fucking hell,*
> *Over there, over there.'*

To the tune of Mary Hopkins' hit of the times, 'Those Were the Days':

> *'Once upon a time there was a north bank*
> *Where we raised a boot or two*
> *And sing away the hours*
> *And think of all the people we would do.*

> *Those were the days my friend*
> *We took the Stretford End*
> *The Shed, the North Bank Highbury*
> *We done the Geordies too*
> *We fight and never lose*
> *Those were the days, oh yes, those were the days*
> *La-la-la-la-la-la, la-la-la-la-la-la (etc.)'*

'The Hokey Cokey' was a good laugh when most of the lads joined in. It went like this:

> *'You put you left boot in, your left boot out,*
> *In, out, in, out, you shake it all about*
> *You kick the fucker's head in and you turn around*
> *And that's what it's all about.*
> *Oh, the hokey cokey (etc.)'*

To the tune of 'Me and My Girl'

> *'The bells are ringing, for the claret and blue*
> *The girls are singing, for the claret and blue.*
> *And when the Hammers are scoring and the money*
> *is pouring*
> *For the claret and blue.*
>
> *No relegation, for the claret and blue,*
> *Just celebration for the claret and blue*
> *And some day we'll win a cup or two*
> *Or three or four or more*
> *For West Ham, and the claret and blue.'*

'Knees Up Mother Brown' was a favourite with us, especially when you had a load on another team's end and we all sang and jumped up and down. It looked unreal and it was great on a tube carriage as well as the carriage would rock back and forth. I imagine you know the words to that. Another old favourite was:

> *'My old man said follow West Ham*
> *And don't dilly dally on the way*
> *Off went the coach with the West Ham on it*

*I followed with scarf and bonnet*
*I dillied and dallied, dallied and dillied*
*Lost me way and don't know where to roam*
*Oh you won't find a team like West Ham United*
*When you can't find your way home.'*

One for Chelsea that has been going for years and still is, sung to the tune of 'We'll Keep the Red Flag Flying Here':
*'From Stamford Bridge, to Upton Park*
*You can stick the blue flag up yer arse.'*

And another one they hated:

*'Blue is their colour*
*Running is their game*
*They're all together and running is their aim*
*So chase them on through the sun and rain*
*Because Chelsea, Chelsea is their name.'*

And, of course, one for the Scousers. There are many versions but this is the original one, to the tune of 'In My Liverpool Home':

*'In your Liverpool home, in your Liverpool home*
*You look in the dustbin for something to eat*
*You find a dead dog and you think it's a treat*
*In your Liverpool home.'*

Even their anthem 'You'll Never Walk Alone' came in for a change:

*'Crawl on crawl on*
*With a knife in your back*

*And you'll never walk again*
*You'll never walk again.'*

One used a few times at Highbury, the name of the tune escapes me:

*'As I was walking down to Highbury*
*Singing singing*
*"West Ham are the champions"*
*I saw Bertie Mee he was standing there*
*All alone all alone*
*I said to Bert, "What's up my friend?"*
*He said, "The North Bank Highbury*
*Ran again"*
*Singing, singing, "West Ham are the champions."'*

This was sung at Ipswich or Norwich or any West Country team:

*'I can't read and I can't write*
*But I can drive a tractor*
*I turn to me left*
*And I turn to my right*
*To drop me fertiliser.'*

You could write a whole book on them, but these are just some of the early ones.

# THE SITES AROUND

## WEST HAM ON THE INTERNET

Without doubt the Internet is a wonderful place for research, emailing people, finding the latest news or joining a supporters club. There are many West Ham clubs online – some good, some bad. The choice is yours.

I have been banned or red-carded by the site moderators of several lists for simply not fitting in. My past was deemed by many to be that of a football thug and, because I had the cheek to disagree or stand up for myself, the red card came out. Some of the lists expect postings to be totally PC, with perfect grammar and spelling, with everyone being perfectly polite to each other. One site even gets upset if you refer to Tottenham fans as 'Yids'. That is not for me!

I have found that the KUMB website is the best around – for Hammer news you can't go past this site. It has a forum you can join or a mailing list, which itself is quite a good laugh. It was started because another West Ham mailing list was deemed too PC for many.

Another list which is good and has loads of USA and overseas Hammers on it is the TOPICA list. Just West Ham talk, no bollocks, and listees will remind you to keep everyday topics that are not West Ham-related off list, which is good as far as I am concerned.

The Bernard Cribbins West Ham list is good as well, and a right laugh. Anything goes on here and if someone joins they must be voted on first by the members. Many of the members have been banned from other lists and are now on this one. Gay Jocks are definitely not tolerated on this list, so if you fall into that group don't bother joining. SIMPLE!

The Intercyber Firm list is a great list. Not ICF, just some West Ham lads who have formed a list. Some may find it too cliquey but it has sensible posters and the odd piss-take. Many listees meet up on match days or travel away together.

The WHO site (WEST HAM ONLINE) is also good and is worth a look.

The 2 Bob site is a site made up of five or so mates who respect each other's opinions and no one else is correct no matter what (it would make a good Totts site, as their fans are never wrong either!). However, there are some lads on there who seem to be connected to the club and now and then a rumour is confirmed. God help you if you don't agree with what someone has written. You get a private email and then you are banned. This has happened to me, although I am now reinstated but I hardly use it at all any more.

I stick with the KUMB site and forum and post on the BCWHL and also the INTERNETCYBER FIRM site, as these sites suit me. I don't get picked on for bad grammar but now and then I get told that I am a shit typist. Fair play, no punches pulled. I agree – I am! We all have one thing in common – WEST HAM. No more or no less. No one is concerned if I left school at eighteen and went to university or have a good office job. I am accepted for what I am, a bricklayer who left school at fourteen and who has been his own boss 95 per cent of his working life.

The opinions I voice here are my own. The best way is to try some of the sites yourself and find out what's best for you and where you feel comfortable. You may be in for a shock. A good contact for those of you outside the UK: ontarioirons@hotmail.com – a club in the Toronto area.

http://groups.yahoo.com/group/bkumb1/
http://groups.yahoo.com/group/BCWHL/
http://gro
http://hammersaway.topcities.com/
WHUFC.co.uk
www.bobbymooreonline.co.uk
http://in-theknow.co.uk
www.sixsixsix.moonfruit.com

# KNEES UP MOTHER BROWN –
# AN ONLINE COMMUNITY
## BY GRAEME HOWLETT

West Ham supporters are a fairly unique breed. Having not attracted any glory hunters since 1966, your average Hammer tends to come from a long line of (long-suffering) supporters, all affected with the same (non-genetic) condition – an unconditional (and often irrational) love for West Ham United Football Club.

My friends, I am one such poor unfortunate. Like many of today's supporters, my parents and their parents before them were all regulars at Upton Park, and all of them were lucky enough to witness the kind of great days that have sadly been only too rare in the last 25 years or so. Those most recent dark days have, however, helped to keep alive that resolute nature and unique spirit of community amongst the faithful followers of West Ham.

My earliest recollection of that community spirit is perhaps a little more recent than some of you (eh, Micky?): sitting aloft my father's shoulders outside a packed East Ham Town Hall on the morning of May 4, 1975 to be precise, watching my boyhood heroes proudly displaying the FA Cup which they had won less than 24 hours earlier thanks to

Sparrow's brace. It's an image that will stay with me always (the throng outside East Ham that is, not Sparrow's gaunt, Bowie-esque features).

My first visit to Upton Park came the following season: predictably, perhaps, we lost. Derby County left the Boleyn victorious on the day thanks to goals from Bruce Rioch and ex-Gooner Charlie George; our consolation goal came from a man who I would be fortunate enough to interview for Knees Up Mother Brown some 25 years later: West Ham and England's Trevor Brooking.

Knees up Mother Brown (or KUMB for short), for those not familiar with our claret-and-blue corner of the world wide web, is currently the longest-running independent Hammers website, having been online since the beginning of the 1997/98 season. Back in those days West Ham was poorly represented on the Internet. The club's own (fledgling) website was pretty much the only regular source of news. Apart from that, one or two pretty basic fan sites (all long gone) were the sum of the Hammers' online presence.

Around that time I was looking for an idea upon which to base a web project. It had to be something I knew a little about so, being a long-suffering West Ham supporter, it seemed a perfect solution to base the website on the team. The idea was to offer something similar to the paper-based fanzines which are sold outside grounds on match day, something that gave the man on the street (or in the Internet café) a say in club matters. An online fanzine, if you like.

All it needed was a name. I wanted something that was representative of the supporters, something traditional yet positive. What better than a terrace favourite sung on the old North Bank away terrace and football special (or Inter City) with equal passion, for many a year? Knees Up Mother Brown it was.

Back then there were still very few people with Internet access, and KUMB was mainly a vessel for a select bunch of supporters to vent their collective spleens (then as now most rants were aimed at our much-loved Board of Directors). Ran initially as a short-term 'project' the site grew steadily and, after a few months, became more of a 'pastime'. As more people joined the online community, so the site grew. Within eighteen months or so KUMB began producing daily news, challenging the official line with regular items – unique then, as now, in that they were written from a supporter's perspective.

That was three years ago now; since then that initial short-term 'project' has become something of a second 'job', consuming more of my spare time than I care to admit. KUMB now has a team of some twenty writers providing material on a regular basis, as well as a mailing list (upon which your author and I first exchanged pleasantries) and forums which receive hundreds of posts from supporters all over the world every day.

In that time I have had the privilege to interview the likes of Frank Lampard and the aforementioned Trevor Brooking, whilst meeting – via the website – some top lads from all over the world, from places as far-flung as Europe, North America and Australia.

Some say that to be a true supporter you have to frequent Upton Park on a regular basis. Having spoken and met with fans like these who travel from various parts of the globe once or twice a year (or more often in some cases) just to get their claret-and-blue fix, I'd have to disagree. In fact, I'd go as far as to say that some of the ex-pats are the most fervent supporters out there. Absence makes the heart grow fonder and all that.

So, even though many of us have moved on from our east

London family roots (I only made it as far as Essex, I hasten to add), the Internet ensures that we can keep our little bit of East End community spirit alive.

And it's that sprit which keeps Knees up Mother Brown going to this day.

*Graeme Howlett, Editor, www.kumb.com*

IN THE KNOW
http://in-theknow.co.uk

Have a look when you are on the net. A great site dealing
with football fans and the culture in general:
www.kumb.com
www.kumb.org.uk
For all your West Ham news, updated daily. An excellent
site for West Ham fans throughout the world.

Also have a look at my site. It's at:
http:/hammersaway.topcities.com/